CLAW YOUR WAY TO THE TOP

How to become the head of a major corporation in roughly a week

Dave Barry

Illustrated by Jerry O'Brien

Rodale Press, Emmaus, Pennsylvania

Printed in the United States of America on acid-free ∞

Book design by Anita G. Patterson

Library of Congress Cataloging in Publication Data
Barry, Dave.
    Claw your way to the top.

    1. Success in business—Anecdotes, facetiae, satire, etc. I. Title.
PN6231.S83B37   1986   818′.5402   86-13013
ISBN 0-87857-652-5   paperback

Distributed in the book trade by St. Martin's Press

     10   paperback

CONTENTS

DEDICATION

This book is dedicated to Burton R. Legume, inventor, who in 1907 dreamed up the concept of the hold button, without which the modern industrial economy would not be possible.

INTRODUCTION

YOU AND THIS BOOK

Maybe you're a young graduate looking for his or her first job. Or maybe you're a veteran employee who'd like to advance up the corporate ladder. Or maybe you're a Labrador retriever who nosed this book off the coffee table, and it fell open to this page.

It makes no difference who you are: the important thing is, this book can show you how to ACHIEVE YOUR CAREER GOALS and WIN THE REWARDS OF SUCCESS such as CARS and HOUSES and GREAT BIG BOATS where, any time you feel like it, you press a little button and UNIFORMED SERVANTS FROM SOME DISEASE-RIDDEN FOREIGN NATION WHERE EVERYBODY IS WRETCHEDLY POOR WHICH IS WHY THEY CAME OVER HERE bring you PLATES OF LITTLE CRACKERS WITH TOASTED CHEESE ON TOP or, if you prefer, RALSTON-PURINA DOG TREATS.

TODAY'S BUSINESS CLIMATE

Today's business climate is partly cloudy with highs in the mid-70s.

Ha ha! That is just a sampler of the kind of snappy humor you will find throughout this book, along with a lot of words printed in capital letters to keep you from falling asleep. Actually, today's business climate is perfect. It is a reaction against the violently anti-business mood that swept the nation back in the sixties, when the young people of America, except for Julie and David Eisenhower, decided to reject money as a life objective and became "hippies." They scorned the corporate world, with its sterility, its greed, its exploitation, its conformity, its Xerox machines that were forever breaking down. They embarked instead upon a quest for a transcendent universal consciousness imbued with peace and love, which they sought to achieve by saying "dude" to members of minority groups and smoking reefers the size of marine flares.

But gradually these young people realized they were paying a subtle price for their counterculture lifestyle, in the sense that they were always waking up in Volkswagen Microbuses with lice in their hair. So they decided that, hey, maybe it wouldn't be so bad to become a sterile conforming greedy exploiter after all, so they went to work for large corporations. Soon they developed children and houses and Volvos, and within a few years they had reached the point of central air-conditioning, from which there is no turning back. Most of them can no longer locate their Grateful Dead albums.

So now everybody except Ralph Nader is strongly pro-business. People who, only a few years back, would have hurled pig blood at Lee Iacocca for some symbolic protest reason or another now think he should run for president. What this means for you is: This is a GREAT TIME for you to get into business. And

1960s PERSON WAKING UP AND REALIZING IT'S TIME TO STOP BEING A HIPPIE AND START MAKING MONEY

don't worry about qualifications: ANYBODY can make it in the business world. All you really need is a little gumption, a willingness to work, some common sense, and a brother-in-law who is Vice-President in Charge of Personnel.

Ha ha! Another business-related joke! This is gonna be some fun, getting you a job, all right!

STEP ONE: SETTING YOUR GOALS

The first step toward your successful business career is to determine your Career Objectives. To do these things, you'll need a nice sharp number-two pencil and some three-by-five cards. I'll wait right here while you go get them, okay? I'll meet you underneath the asterisks on the next page! Hurry back! This is going to be exciting!

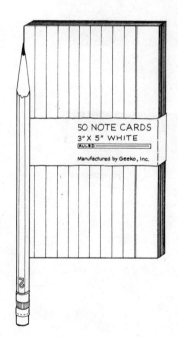

(Brief pause.)

The point of the preceding paragraph, obviously, was to get rid of the totally hopeless dweebs who actually think they need three-by-five cards to determine their Career Objectives. These are the same people who you just know are going to write down things like:

1. I would like to work with people.

Which of course is a joke, because it is a proven fact that the more you work with people, the more you hate them. Look at the clerks at any big-city Bureau of Motor Vehicles: They work with people all day long, and their basic approach to human interaction is to make you wait in line as long as possible and then tell you you're in the wrong line, in hopes that you'll have a very painful and ultimately fatal seizure, and they'll get to watch.

So you savvy persons have ruled out "working with people" as a Career Objective. What you want, from your career, is a SENSE OF FULFILLMENT AS A HUMAN BEING and MAXIMUM PERSONAL SATISFACTION as measured in U.S. DOLLARS. You want a Rolex watch and numerous fast cars. You want employees so desperate for your approval that you could put your cigar out on their foreheads and they'd thank you. You want to be able to leave Supreme Court justices on "hold" for upwards of an hour. And you know that you do not get these things by diddling around with three-by-five cards.

*   *   *

Welcome back! Got your cards? Great! Now first, I'd like you to write down, on each card, a Career Objective, such as "working with people." Okay? I want you to do this until you have listed 800 Career Objectives—you might have to go get some more cards!—and then I want you to arrange them in order according to which objective contains the most vowels, okay? Great! We're on our way! Call me when you're done!

TEST YOUR BUSINESS I.Q.

1. You are the world's largest manufacturer of carbonated beverages, and you have a product that is famous worldwide, that is virtually synonymous with the term "soft drink," and that has had the same formula for 99 years. It has a very loyal following. You are making millions and millions of dollars selling it. You should:

(a) Just keep it the way it is.
(b) Change the formula.
(c) Set fire to your own hair.

CORRECT ANSWER: Either *(b)* or *(c)*.

2. You are a major defense contractor, and you are building a gun for the Army that is supposed to be able to shoot down enemy planes. So far the taxpayers have paid you nearly $2 billion for it, and all your tests indicate that the only way it would have any negative effect on an enemy plane is if you could somehow sneak into the cockpit and manually whack the pilot over the head with it. How should you deal with this problem?

(a) You should try really hard to do a better job.
(b) You should tell the Defense Department that they probably should get another contractor.
(c) You should refund at least some of the taxpayers' money.

CORRECT ANSWER: What problem?

3. You are a major automobile manufacturer. You have been losing sales to cars from other nations, particularly Japan, because their cars tend to be fuel efficient, technologically advanced, and extremely well made, whereas the most innovative concept you have come up with in the past two decades is the opera window. You should:

(a) Have Congress pass a law restricting Japanese imports, so consumers will have no choice but to buy your cars.

(b) Have Congress pass a law making it legal for you to kidnap consumers' children and not return them until the consumers buy your cars.
(c) Have Congress pass a law ordering the United States Army to barge directly into consumers' homes and take their money at gunpoint and give it to you.
(d) Remind everybody a lot about Pearl Harbor.

CORRECT ANSWER: These are all pretty good.

4. You are in charge of a large department, and you have an opening for a supervisor. The two obviously best-qualified candidates are women who have worked in the department for the same amount of time. Both are intelligent, highly competent, and respected by the other employees. In every way they seem equally qualified, although it happens that one of them is black. What decision do you make?

(a) You promote the black woman, on the theory that it will help compensate for past injustices.
(b) You promote the white woman, on the theory that if you promote the black woman, people will say it was just because she's black.
(c) You flip a coin.

CORRECT ANSWER: You promote a man.

HOW TO SCORE
Give yourself one point for each close friend you have in the Personnel Department.

Chapter One

THE HISTORY OF BUSINESS

When we look around us at the modern world, we see businesses everywhere, unless of course we happen to be, for example, in the bathroom. But even there, we see EVIDENCE of a thriving industrial economy, such as the Ty-D-Bowl automatic commode freshener. Sitting there and thinking about it, you have to marvel at the incredible creativity and diversity of the business world. Where did all of this come from? How did the human race get from the point of being primitive and stupid to the point where it could automatically, without lifting a finger, turn its toilet water blue? Let's see if we can answer some of these questions. My guess is we can't.

THE VERY FIRST BUSINESSES

Many, many years ago, there was no business on Earth. This is because the Earth was primarily molten lava, which is not a good economic climate. Office furniture would melt in a matter of seconds.

Then the Earth started to cool, and tiny one-celled animals—the amigo, the paramedic, the rotarian—began to form. Over the course of several million years, these animals learned to join together to form primitive corporations, called "jellyfish," which were capable of only the most basic business activities, such as emitting waste and eating lunch. By today's standards, these corporations were very unsophisticated: if, for example, you mentioned the phrase "Dow Jones Industrial Average" to them, they would have no idea what you were talking about. They would probably sting you.

DID DINOSAURS HAVE BUSINESSES?

Nobody can really say for sure, because the Ice Age destroyed all their records. But paleontologists now believe that, yes, dinosaurs probably did have businesses. Not the Brontosaurus, of course. That would be ridiculous. How would he hold his briefcase? But the Tyrannosaurus Rex has those funny little arms, which would have been perfect (see diagram at left). Paleontologists think he was probably in Sales.

PRIMITIVE HUMAN BUSINESSES

When primitive humans first came along, they did not engage in business as we now think of it. They engaged in squatting around in caves naked. This went on for, I would say, roughly two or three million years, when all of a sudden a primitive person, named Oog, came up with an idea. "Why not," he said, "pile thousands of humongous stones on top of each other in the desert to form great big geometric shapes?" Well, everybody thought this was an absolutely *terrific* idea, and soon they were hard at work. It wasn't until several thousand years later that they realized they had been suckered into a classic "pyramid" scheme, and of course by that time, Oog was in the Bahamas.

BUSINESS DURING THE MIDDLE AGES

Business during the Middle Ages was slow. The main job opportunity available was serf, which involved whacking at the soil with a stick. It was not the kind of work where you had a lot of room for advancement. The best a serf could hope for, if he was really good at it, was that he would be rewarded by not having one of his arms sliced off by a passing knight.

If you wanted to be a knight you had to know somebody, and it really wasn't that much better than being a serf. You were always being sent off to try to get the Holy Land back from the Turks. This was no fun at all, because of course the Holy Land is very sunny, meaning your armor would get hot enough to fry an egg on. In fact the Turks, who dressed in light, casual, 100 percent cotton garments, would often do this. They'd sneak up behind a knight and crack an egg on his armor, then race away, laughing in Turkish, before he could turn around. So as you can imagine, knights would come back in a pretty bad mood, and often would have to slice off several serf arms before they even wanted to *talk* about it.

So the bottom line is that the Middle Ages were hardly the kind of ages where anybody wanted to make any long-term business commitments. All the really smart investors were waiting for the Renaissance.

THE RENAISSANCE

The Renaissance was caused by Leonardo da Vinci, who drew the first primitive sketches of what would eventually become the helicopter. Of course, nobody really understood the significance of this at the time. But people did realize that, whatever this new invention was, it was going to require a tremendous amount of insurance. Thus a major business was born.

This was followed by trade with the Orient. The way this worked was, Europeans would gather up some gold, and they would tromp across Asia to the Orient, where they would trade their gold for spices. They didn't really *want* spices, you understand, but the Orientals claimed that spice was all they had, and the Europeans, having tromped all that way, wanted to take home *something*.

After some years of this, the Europeans were starting to run out of gold. Also their food was so heavily spiced that it glowed in the dark. They probably would have all died of heartburn if Columbus had not discovered the New World.

THE BIRTH OF THE HELICOPTER

THE NEW WORLD

Every schoolchild is familiar with the story of how Columbus set off in three tiny ships (the *Pinto,* the *Cordoba,* and the *Coupe de Ville*), and right away his crew started getting very nauseous and asking why for God's sake he had decided on three *tiny* ships instead of one *medium* ship. Nevertheless Columbus pressed on, ignoring popular fears that he would sail off the edge of the Earth, and finally he and his hardy band made it to the New World, except for the *Pinto,* which mysteriously exploded, and the *Cordoba,* which due to a navigational error actually *did* sail off the edge of the Earth.

The New World had an extremely good business climate. For one thing, there was plenty of land, and nobody owned it, unless you counted the people who had been living there for several thousand years. For another thing, it had an abundance of the two crucial factors you need for economic development: Water Power, in the form of rivers, and Raw Materials, in the form of ore. So soon millions of Europeans flocked over to the New World to make their fortunes. They stood around all day, sunup to sundown, throwing handfuls of ore into the rivers and waiting for economic development to take place. They would have starved to death if a friendly Indian named Squanto (which is Indian for "Native American") hadn't come along and shown them how to plant corn. "You put the seeds in the ground," explained Squanto. He couldn't believe what kind of morons he was dealing with.

Soon the corn came up, and the Europeans decided to celebrate by inviting all the Indians over for a big Thanksgiving dinner, then sending them off to live on reservations in North Dakota.

THE RISE OF THE MODERN CORPORATION

At the beginning of the modern corporate era, many businesses actually made things. Typically, they'd get hold of a Raw Material, which they'd smelt and pour into a mold, where it would cool and form a product, which they'd sell for a profit, which the owner would use to buy his family a nice house on Long Island.

The problem was that when the owner died, the family members were darned if they'd come in off Long Island and engage in anything as filthy as smelting, so they'd hire a professional manager to run the business. Often, however, the professional manager was a graduate of Harvard Business School, and consequently *he* wasn't exactly dying to smelt either. So he'd dream up other corporate activities for himself to engage in, such as Marketing, Long-Range Planning, Management by Objectives, and Lunch, and he'd hire additional managers, who of course would turn right around and hire managers of their own, and so on.

This is how we arrived at the modern corporation, where at the very top you have a chief executive who spends his entire day posing for Annual Report photographs and testifying before Congress; and beneath him you have several thousand executives engaged in "middle management," which is the corporate term for "management activities in which there is no possible way for anybody to tell whether you're screwing up"; and beneath them you have tens of thousands of secretarial, clerical, and reception personnel; and beneath *them,* somewhere in a factory nobody ever goes to because there is no decent place around it where you can have lunch, you have the actual production work force, which consists of a grizzled old veteran employee named "Bud."

This modern corporate system offers something for everybody:

• THE EXECUTIVES get enormous salaries and bonuses and stock options and offices big enough to play jai alai in.

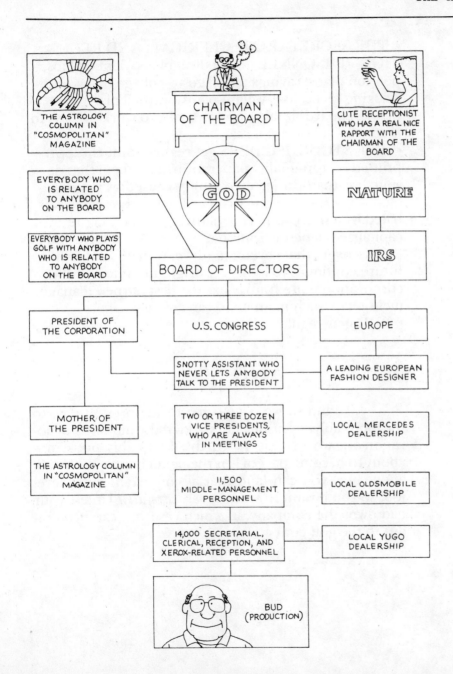

• THE SECRETARIAL, CLERICAL, AND RECEP-TION PERSONNEL get medical plans, dental plans, pension plans, savings plans, go-to-college plans, stop-smoking plans, lose-weight plans, softball plans, and bulletin boards it takes upwards of two working days to read.

• THE STOCKHOLDERS get regular annual reports printed on top-quality paper informing them that despite less-than-projected earnings caused by impossi-ble-to-foresee foreign-currency fluctuations exacer-bated by a short-term restructuring of the long-term capitalized debenturization of the infrastructure and the discovery that certain moths may mate for life, the future continues to look very bright inasmuch as the corporation quite frankly has the best darned manage-ment team the human mind can conceive of.

• BUD gets regular five-minute breaks.

AND SO . . .

. . . and so we have come to the present day, to the incredibly sophisticated world of the modern corpo-ration—a world that YOU, thanks to this book, are about to become part of! In the next chapter, we'll talk about how you can land that all-important entry-level job, so you'll want to study it *very carefully!* Unless your dad owns the company, in which case you can head on out to the golf course.

Chapter Two

GETTING A JOB

In this chapter, we'll take you step-by-step through the job-hunting process, starting right at the beginning.

BIRTH

This is the time to start preparing for your business career. You can bet your little navel protuberance that the *other* babies are preparing, and you don't want to fall so far behind that they wind up as vice-presidents and you wind up serving them food and wearing a comical white hat in the corporate cafeteria. In fact, I'd recommend that you start preparing *before* birth, except that you'd have trouble seeing the flashcards.

The flashcard procedure is as follows: you lie on your back in your crib, and your parents lean over you and hold up cards, each of which has printed on it a basic fact that will help you succeed in business.

As your parents show you the card, they should read it out loud in a perky voice, as though they are just having the time of their lives, and you should indicate comprehension by waving your arms and pooping.

You should spend as much time with the flash-cards as possible. Ideally, you'll reach adolescence without ever once getting an unobstructed view of your parents' faces. As an adult, you'll carry around a little wallet card that says "7 × 9 = 63," because it will remind you of Mother.

PRESCHOOL

Look for a strong pre-business curriculum, one that emphasizes practical activities, such as blocks, over liberal-arts activities, such as gerbils.

ELEMENTARY SCHOOL

This is where you should learn to add, subtract, multiply, and divide, which are skills that are essential for filling out expense reports; you should also develop lifelong chumships with anybody whose name ends in "II," or, even better, "III." You might also consider learning to read. This is not really necessary, of course, inasmuch as you will have a secretary for this purpose, but some businesspersons like to occasionally do it themselves for amusement on long airplane trips.

HIGH SCHOOL

The point of high school is to get yourself into a good college. The way you do this is by being well rounded, which is measured by how many organizations you belong to. Many college admissions officers select students by actually slapping a ruler down on the list of accomplishments underneath each applicant's high school yearbook picture. So you should join every one of the ludicrous high school organizations available to you, such as the Future Appliance Owners Club and the National Honor Society. If they won't let you into the National Honor Society, have your parents file a lawsuit alleging discrimination on the basis of intelligence.

Another thing you need to do in high school is get good SAT scores, which are these two numbers you receive in the mail from the Educational Testing Service in Princeton, New Jersey. They have a whole warehouse filled with numbers up there. To get yours, you have to send some money off by mail to Princeton, then you have to go sit in a room full of other students with number-two pencils and answer questions like "BRAZIL is to COMPENSATE as LUST is to. . . ." Then you have to look at the various multiple choices and try to figure out what kind of mood the folks up at the Educational Testing Service were in on the day they made up that particular question.

Nobody has the vaguest idea anymore how this elaborate ritual got started, what it has to do with anything in the real world, or how the Educational Testing Service decides what numbers to send you. My personal theory is that it has to do with how much money you send them in the mail. I think the amounts they tell you to send are actually just Suggested Minimum Donations, if you get my drift.

COLLEGE

College is basically a large group of buildings, usually separated by lawns, where you go to major in business. This means you must avoid:

• Courses where you have to trace the Development of something, such as the Novel.

• Courses that involve numbers that cannot be categorized as debits or credits, such as "square roots."
• Courses involving a foreign language, such as French (this also includes courses involving funny-sounding English, like in those old plays where everybody is always saying: "Whatst? Dost thou sittest upon mine horst? Egad!" etc.).
• Any course involving maps, the Renaissance, or specific dates such as "1066."
• Any course where you sit around a classroom trying to figure out what the hell Truth is.

What you want to take are courses that have the word "Business" in them somewhere, such as Introduction to Business, Getting to Know Business a Little Better, Kissing Business Right on the Lips, etc.

GRADUATE SCHOOL

There are advantages and disadvantages to going to graduate school. The main advantage is that if you go to a really good graduate school, like Harvard, you'll have a very easy time finding a good job. At night, as you lie in your bed, your window will often be broken by stones, around which have been wrapped lucrative offers. The main disadvantage is that you couldn't get admitted to Harvard even if you held the dean's wife at gunpoint. So I think you're better off applying for a job.

ARE THERE JOBS AVAILABLE?

Heck yes! Don't you listen to those Negative Nellies who tell you there aren't any good jobs anymore, just because the steel, automobile, shoe, clothing, railroad, and agricultural industries have all collapsed! There are new career opportunities opening up all the time in today's fast-changing economy. Just to give you an idea, let's look at

LOBSTER REPAIR: A FAST-GROWING FIELD

You know how, when you go into a seafood restaurant, they have the lobsters up front, in a tank, all trying to scuttle back out of the way and hide under each other so they won't get eaten? Well, it's inevitable that some lobsters get damaged in the process—broken claws, eye stalks falling off, that kind of thing. And then you have the problem that (a) you have damaged lobsters, which you can't serve to your customers and (b) you have these loose random eye stalks lying around the bottom of your tank, which hardly act as a Cheerful Greeting to your incoming customers. This is why there is such a tremendous demand today for people who know how, using modern adhesives, to reassemble a damaged lobster, or use the leftover parts to construct a whole *new* one, often incorporating a new and improved design ("Hey," more than one delighted restaurant patron has cried recently. "My lobster has a claw made entirely out of eye stalks!").

And this is just *one* new emerging-growth career field. Others include: Drug Overlord; Computer Geek; Televised Christian; Person Who Sells Staples to the Defense Department for What It Cost to Liberate France; Vigilante; and Pip, whose job is to stand behind Gladys Knight and go "whooo whooo" at certain points during the song, "Midnight Train to Georgia."

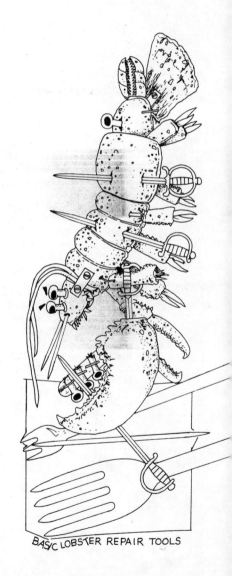

BASIC LOBSTER REPAIR TOOLS

WHERE SHOULD YOU BEGIN YOUR JOB SEARCH?

WELDER WANTED — To weld certain pieces of metal together.

The answer to that question is right in your local newspaper. That's right! Every day, hundreds of employers pay good money to advertise jobs in the classified ad section, apparently unaware that practically nobody reads it! So I want you to turn to the help wanted section right now and locate all the ads that look promising.

The way to do this is to count the adjectives. For example, take the ads shown at left.

The first ad contains only one adjective, and thus represents a poor career opportunity. The second ad, on the other hand, clearly offers a very exciting opportunity, based on the adjective count.

ADMINISTRATIVE ASSISTANT
Young-thinking, fast-moving, forward-looking emerging-growth company with dynamic, attractive plant-filled lobby featuring modernistic, incomprehensible sculpture and old, heavily thumbed issues of *Pork Buyer Weekly* seeks eager, ambitious, personable, aggressive, can-do, confident, hard-driving, highly motivated self-starter to clean scum-encrusted office coffee-related implements.

YOUR RESUME

Your resume is more than just a piece of paper: it is a piece of paper with lies written all over it. Often, a good resume can mean the difference between not getting a job and not even coming close.

In writing your resume, you should follow the format shown in the example on page 15, although you might want to modify it to suit your individual situation. For example, you may want to use your own name, instead of the word "NAME." Unless you have a name like "Dewey."

A lot of people make a really stupid mistake, namely, they send their resume to the Personnel Department. Pay close attention here: NEVER SEND ANYTHING TO THE PERSONNEL DEPARTMENT.

RESUME

NAME: (Last name first, first name in
         the middle, middle name way off
         to the right, in a little box.
         Should sound British.)

ADDRESS: (Include clear directions as to
         how to get there, such as, "If
         you come to a Dairy Queen on your
         left, you have gone too far.")

PHONE: (Specify whether "Princess" or
         "Standard" model; note any special
         features such as "last number re-
         dial.")

CAREER OBJECTIVE: (This should sound like
the speeches given by Miss America contes-
tants to demonstrate that they have a Per-
sonality. For example: "I would very much
like to utilize my skills to the greatest
of my ability in hopes of achieving a sig-
nificant degree of accomplishment." Leave
out the part about hoping someday to work
with handicapped animals.)

SUMMARY OF CAREER ACCOMPLISHMENTS: (The
important thing here is verbs. Verbs verbs
verbs! You want to sound like a person with
a slightly overactive thyroid. Be vague.
Lie. Remember that nobody's going to read
this.)

    September, 1985 to present: ADMINISTRATOR.
    Initiate, coordinate, participate,
    and eliminate all traces of long-

and short-term mid-range interim
approaches.

1983 to 1985: COORDINATOR.
Gathered, analyzed, and collated
a wide range of data, then kneaded
it on a floured surface and baked
it in a moderate oven until a tooth-
pick inserted in the center came
out clean. Served six.
REASON FOR LEAVING: Communists.

1981 to 1983: ASSOCIATE.
Put my right hand in, took my right
hand out, did the hokey-pokey, and
shook it all about.
REASON FOR LEAVING: Ennui.

EDUCATION

GRADUATE SCHOOL: Harvard and Yale University
School of Learning, Ph.D. in Business Appliance Management, 1980.

COLLEGE: Fargo and Surrounding Farms College
of Arts and Sciences Such as Long Division,
B.M. in Restaurant Communications, 1978.

REFERENCES

I should be happy to supply the names of any
number of deceased grade-school teachers upon
request.

The absolute last thing the people in Personnel want the
company to do is hire you. They don't want the company to hire *anybody,* because it just means more work
for them. As far as Personnel is concerned, every new
employee is one more cretin who will never learn how to
fill out his medical and dental claim forms correctly.

So if you send your resume to Personnel, they'll set fire to it immediately and send you back the following letter:

Dear (YOUR NAME):

Thank you so very, very much for sending us your resume. What a nice surprise it was! "Look at this," the mail person cried as we all gathered 'round. "(YOUR NAME) has been so kind as to send us his or her resume!" What excitement there was, here in Personnel! We danced far into the night!

Sadly, however, we do not expect to have any positions available until approximately the end of time. We will, however, keep the remains of your resume on file, in a tasteful urn, and you may rest assured that nobody will disturb it except for routine dusting.

Sincerely,

The Personnel Department

LG:pu

So the question becomes: what do you do with your resume? My advice is, set fire to it yourself. Nobody ever reads resumes anyway. I only told you to write one because it's an old jobseeker tradition, and we have so few traditions left.

Good! We've taken care of that! Now let's move on to the next step, which is. . .

WRITING
AN EFFECTIVE LETTER
THAT WILL GET YOU
A JOB INTERVIEW

In an ideal world, of course, your letter would say, "Dear Sir or Madam: Give me a job interview or I will kill your spouse."

But we do not live in an ideal world. We live in a world that has strict postal regulations regarding what you can say in letters. So you're going to have to take the "soft sell" approach to getting an interview. Chances are, you've already written such a letter, and chances are it sounds something like this:

```
Dear Sirs or Madams:

As a dynamic, eager, hardworking young
person who brings an enormous quantity
of enthusiasm to every task, on account
of being so eager, I am writing to ex-
press my sincere desire to be considered
for the position of Employee within your
company.  I am confident that once we
have had a chance at some mutual and con-
venient time to meet and shake hands
firmly while making eye contact and re-
viewing all my major accomplishments
dating back to the birth canal, you will
realize how mutually beneficial it would
be for your firm and myself to seek some
means of achieving our future goals in
a way that would benefit both parties.
Mutually.  I shall contact your office
by telephone every seven or eight min-
utes, starting this morning, to determine
a time that would be mutual and dynamic
for you.


Very sincerely,

Byron B. Buffington II

Byron B. Buffington II
```

The advantage of this kind of letter is that it has a confident, positive, assertive, enthusiastic tone. The disadvantage is that it makes you sound like the biggest jerk ever to roam the planet. I mean, look at it from the perspective of the people at the company: they have to actually *work* with the people they hire, and nobody is going to want to work with a little rah-rah snotface.

What you want is a job application letter that makes you sound like a regular person, somebody who would be fun to work with:

```
Hey--

So the priest says to the rabbi, he
says, "But how do you get the snake to
wear lipstick?" Ha ha! Get it? Say,
did you get a load of the new clerk in
Accounts Receivable? Whoooo! She is so
ugly, it takes two men and a strong dog
just to look at her! Ha ha! How about
those Giants? I don't know about you,
but I say we knock off early today.


Take it easy,

Byron "The Buffer" Buffington
```

WHOM YOU SHOULD SEND YOUR LETTER TO

A vice-president. It makes no difference which one. All vice-presidents do exactly the same thing with their mail, namely write the first name of a middle-management subordinate in the upper right-hand corner, followed by a question mark, like this: "Dan?" They do this by reflex action to everything placed in front of them, usually without reading it, then they toss it into the "OUT" basket. If an employee is hospitalized and a get-well card is passed around the company, it usually winds up with an unintelligible blot in the upper right-hand corner where all the vice-presidents wrote the names of subordinates followed by question marks.

Nobody will ever dare throw your letter away, once a vice-president has written on it. Eventually somebody is going to ask you to come in for an interview, if only to find out how the snake joke starts.

HOW TO PREPARE
FOR YOUR JOB INTERVIEW

One obvious way to remain calm and perspiration free during an interview, of course, is narcotics, but there you run into the problem of scratching yourself and trying to steal things off the interviewer's desk. So as a precaution, what most veteran employment counselors recommend is that you wear "dress shields," which, as some of you women already know, are these highly absorbent devices that you stuff into your armpits. They are available in bulk at any good employment agency. For a job interview, you should stuff three or four shields into each pit. This will cause your arms to stick out from your body at an odd angle, so to prevent your interviewer from attaching any significance to this, you want to begin the interview with a casual remark, as is illustrated by the following "model" interview dialog:

INTERVIEWER: Hello, Bob. Nice to meet you.
YOU: There's nothing odd about *my* arms!

THE INTERVIEW PROCESS

Basically, what the interviewer wants to know is how well you can "think on your feet." So what he'll try to do, with his questions, is throw you some "curve balls," which means you should come to the interview well supplied with snappy retorts. Let's go back to our "model" interview:

INTERVIEWER: Tell me, Bob, why are you interested in coming to work for us?
YOU: Who wants to know?
INTERVIEWER: Ha ha! Got me there! Bob, what specific strengths do you feel you would bring to this job?
YOU: So's your old man!
INTERVIEWER (tears of laughter streaming down his face):   Bob, you sound like the kind of quick-thinking employee we are looking for! How about a large starting salary?
YOU: You and what army?

CONGRATULATIONS

You've got the job! In the next chapter, you'll learn how to figure out what exactly the nature of this job is—specifically, whether it involves any duties, and if so, how you can get out of them.

Chapter Three

HOW TO DO YOUR JOB, WHATEVER IT IS

To really succeed in a business or organization, it is sometimes helpful to know what your job is, and whether it involves any duties. Try to find this out in your first couple of weeks by asking around among your co-workers. "Hi," you should say. "I'm Byron Buffington, a new employee! What's the name of my job?" If they answer Long-Range Planner or Lieutenant Governor, you are pretty much free to lounge around and do crossword puzzles until retirement. Most other jobs, however, will involve some work.

There are two major kinds of work in the modern corporation or organization:

1. Taking phone messages for people who are in meetings; and

2. Going to meetings.

Your ultimate career strategy will be to get to a job involving primarily number two, going to meetings, as soon as possible, because that's where the real prestige is. But most corporations and organizations like to start everybody out with a couple of years of taking messages, so we'll discuss this important basic business skill first.

TAKING A PHONE MESSAGE

When the phone rings, lift the receiver, punch whichever button is lit, and say: "Thank you for calling the Marketing Department (or whatever). Kindly hold the line." Then quickly punch the hold button.

Now you should check around briefly to make sure that everybody the caller could possibly want to talk to is in a meeting. This is also a good time to go to the bathroom. When you return, punch the hold button again, and say: "I am sorry, but whomever the person is to whom you wish to speak is in a meeting at this present time and is expected to remain there until at least the next major economic recession. Did you wish to leave a message?"

Now this is very important: the *instant* the caller starts to respond, you must say: "Will you please hold again for a moment?" and punch the hold button with a very rapid and sure motion. Now you should head on down to the Supplies Cabinet and get some handy preprinted phone message forms, in case the caller did wish to leave a message.

When you get back to the desk, push the button again and say, "I am sorry. Now, did you wish to leave a message?" And the caller will say something like, "Listen, I'm calling from France and I don't *want* Marketing, so could you ask the operator to transfer. . . ."

Now at this point, if you are an experienced message-taker, your sixth sense tells you the caller is *just about to complete a sentence,* and we certainly don't want *that* to happen! So you will have to very quickly—but politely!—ask the caller to please hold the line again for a moment, and at the same time strike the hold button the way a hungry cobra strikes a small furry mammal.

Okay, we're almost ready to take the actual message. Punch the button again, and say (in case the caller has forgotten): "Thank you for calling the Marketing Department! How may we help you?" Now at this point, there is every likelihood that the caller will have hung up. This might seem like a major obstacle, in terms of being able to take a message, but it is not, thanks to the handy preprinted phone message forms that you got from the Supplies Cabinet. Here is what they look like:

WHILE YOU WERE OUT IN A MEETING

Mr./Mrs./Miss/
Ms./Rev./Massa/ _____
(name)

Check one:

( ) Telephoned.
( ) Did not telephone.
( ) Thought about telephoning, but then changed his or her mind.
( ) Telephoned, but could not for the LIFE of him or her remember why.
( ) Telephoned, then hung right up, but I am certain it was him or her.
( ) Wants you to call and attempt to leave a message for him or her.
( ) Wants to fire you.
( ) Wants to reveal a sordid episode from his or her past involving a goat.
( ) Wants to end World Hunger in our lifetime.
( ) Wants your body.
( ) Wants for nothing.
( ) Wants to tell you the joke about the man who finds out he has only eight hours to live, so he goes home and makes love with his wife once, twice, three times, and finally they fall asleep, and at 3 A.M. he tries to wake her up, and she says, "Not AGAIN! Some of us have to get up in the morning!"
( ) Ate paste as a child.
( ) Has the clap.

So all you have to do is check the appropriate space to indicate what message you feel the caller would have left if he or she had had the time. The only hard part is deciding what name you put where it says "name." I recommend you put the name of a corporate vice-president, for two reasons:

1. It will enhance your reputation as a person who has spoken directly to a vice-president; and

2. Nobody will ever be able to prove that you're wrong. Any attempt to contact the vice-president about his "message" will result in failure, because he will of course be in a meeting.

Okay. It is all very well and good to be able to take phone messages, but you are never going to get to a position of corporate power, a position where you can cost thousands of people their jobs with a single bone-head decision, until you learn how to attend meetings.

THE CORPORATE MEETING

It might be useful to compare the modern corporate meeting to a football huddle, in which the people attending the meeting are a "team," attempting to come up with a "play" in which each team member will be assigned responsibility to "block" a specific "defender" so that a "fullback" will be able to carry the ball through a "hole" in the "line" and get into the "end zone" for a "touchdown," which will cause everybody to exchange "high-five" handshakes and slap each other on the "butt." So we can see that in fact it is not at all useful to compare a modern corporate meeting to a football huddle. It was a pretty stupid idea, and I apologize for it.

Perhaps a better analogy would be to compare the modern corporate meeting to a funeral, in the sense that you have a gathering of people who are wearing uncomfortable clothing and would rather be somewhere else. The major differences are that:

1. Usually only one or two people get to talk at a funeral; and

2. Most funerals have a definite purpose (to say nice things about a dead person) and reach a definite conclusion (this person is put in the ground), whereas meetings generally drone on until the legs of the highest-ranking person present fall asleep.

Also, nothing is ever really buried in a meeting. An idea may *look* dead, but it will always reappear at another meeting later on. If you have ever seen the movie *Night of the Living Dead,* you have a rough idea how modern corporations and organizations operate, with projects and proposals that everybody thought were killed constantly rising from their graves to stagger back into meetings and eat the brains of the living.

HOW TO ACT IN A MEETING

This depends on what kind of meeting it is. There are two major kinds:

1. MEETINGS THAT ARE HELD FOR BASICALLY THE SAME REASON THAT ARBOR DAY IS OBSERVED, namely, tradition. For example, a lot of managerial people like to meet on Monday, because it is Monday. You'll get used to it. You'd better, because this kind of meeting accounts for 83 percent of all meetings

held (based on a study in which I wrote down numbers until one of them looked about right).

This kind of meeting operates the way "Show and Tell" operates in nursery school, with everybody getting to say something, the difference being that in nursery school the kids actually have something new to say. When it's your turn, you should say you're still working on whatever it is you're supposed to be working on. This may seem pretty dumb, since *obviously* you'd be working on whatever you're supposed to be working on, and even if you weren't, you'd *claim* you were, but this is the traditional thing for everybody to say. It would be a lot faster if the person running the meeting would just say, "Everybody who is still working on whatever he or she is supposed to be working on, raise your hand!" You'd all be out of there in five minutes, even allowing time for jokes. But this is not how we do it in America. My guess is, it's how they do it over in Japan.

2. MEETINGS WHERE THERE IS SOME ALLEGED PURPOSE. These are trickier, because what you do depends on what the purpose is. Sometimes the purpose is harmless, like somebody wants to show everybody slides of pie charts and give everybody a copy of a big fat report. All you have to do in this kind of meeting is sit there and have elaborate sexual fantasies, then take the report back to your office and throw it away, unless of course you're a vice-president, in which case you write the name of a subordinate in the upper right-hand corner, followed by a question mark, like this: "Norm?" Then you send it to Norm and forget all about it (although it will plague old Norm for the rest of his career).

But sometimes you go to meetings where the purpose is to get your "input" on something. This is very serious, because what it means is, they want to make sure that in case whatever it is turns out to be stupid or fatal, you'll get some of the blame. I mean, if they thought it was any good, they wouldn't want your "input," would they? So you have to somehow escape from the meeting before they get around to asking you anything. One way is to set fire to your tie. Another is to have an accomplice interrupt the meeting and announce that you have a phone call from somebody very important, such as the president of the company, or the Pope. It should be either one or the other. It would sound fishy if the accomplice said, "You have a call from the president of the company. Or the Pope."

A FUN THING TO DO IF SOMEBODY FALLS ASLEEP IN A MEETING

Have everybody leave the room, then collect a group of total strangers, from right off the street, and have them sit around the sleeping person and stare at him until he wakes up. Then have one of them say to him, in a very somber voice, "Bob, your plan is very, very risky, but you've given us no choice but to try it. I only hope, for your sake, that you know what the hell you're getting yourself into." Then they should file quietly from the room.

HOW TO TAKE NOTES DURING A MEETING

Use a yellow legal pad. At the top, write the date and underline it twice:

October 8

Now wait until an important person such as your boss starts talking. When he does, look at him with a look of enraptured interest, as though he is revealing the secrets of life itself. Then write interlocking rectangles, like this:

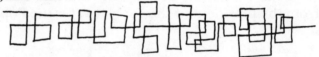

If it is an especially lengthy meeting, you can try something like this:

After a while, you will want to fill in any holes in the date:

October 8

Also, if you're sitting next to somebody you can trust, you can use your notepad to discuss various other people at the meeting:

EL DORKO

SPECIAL NOTE OF ENCOURAGEMENT
TO TIMID HOUSEWIVES
WHO HAVE BEEN THINKING ABOUT
MAYBE TRYING TO GET INTO
THE BUSINESS WORLD BUT ARE
WORRIED THAT IT MIGHT BE
TOO HARD AND THEY MIGHT NOT BE
QUALIFIED TO DO ANYTHING
EXCEPT MAKE TUNA CASSEROLE

Boy, are YOU ever in for a surprise. I mean, here you have been staying home, day after day, cooking meals and doing the laundry and praising the primitive refrigerator art your children produce and scrubbing away at the advanced fungal growths around the base of the toilet, during which time your husband has been GONE. And when he gets home, all he has the energy to do is just COLLAPSE on the Barca-Lounger and talk about what a DIFFICULT DAY he has had because the ACCOUNTS RECEIVABLE (whatever *that* is) won't "BALANCE" (whatever *that* means). So you have naturally come to believe that whatever goes on in the business world must be just DEATHLY difficult and complex, to cause a grown man such ANGUISH.

Well, just you wait until, following the program outlined in this book, you get your first actual job in business. You are going to think you died and went straight to heaven. For one thing, everybody there is a GROWNUP. They allow NO CHILDREN in business. You never have to take ANYBODY, for any reason, to the potty. Speaking of which, if a business toilet gets dirty, you just CALL MAINTENANCE ON THE PHONE, and THEY COME AND CLEAN IT! And if they don't, YOU CAN WRITE A SNOTTY MEMO-RANDUM ABOUT IT!

And the best part of it is—as you will see, once we get into how businesses work—YOU NEED NO SPECIAL SKILLS OR QUALIFICATIONS TO BE PART OF A BUSINESS. All you have to do is figure out what simple concept the other people are really talking about when they use their complex business terms. For example, when your husband says the "Accounts Receivable" won't "balance," what he means is, he has these two NUMBERS that are supposed to be the SAME, but instead they're DIFFERENT. Is that pathetic, or what? I mean, really, would you call that a PROBLEM? Especially if you compare it with, say, a situation where you're at the shopping mall Burger King and you have finally managed to get your food and your children and your packages to a table, and just as you start to bite into your Whopper Junior, your two-year-old knocks his chocolate milk onto a priest, your six-year-old commences projectile vomiting and your four-year-old wanders off, enraptured, in the company of a toothless man with needle marks and Nazi tattoos. Now THIS is what I would call a PROBLEM, and you have to deal with it ALL BY YOURSELF. Meanwhile, back at "work," your husband is drinking nice hot coffee in a nice clean vomit-free office, fretting about his two little NUMBERS with the aid of a COMPUTER and probably three or four CO-WORKERS, all of whom will eventually go have a nice quiet lunch featuring MARGARITAS and NO CHILDREN.

So trust me, housewives. You'll do FINE in the business world. Your husband does, right? How hard can it be?

Chapter Four

STEPPING OVER YOUR CO-WORKERS

Okay. Now you can take phone messages. You can go to meetings. In short, you can do everything that can be reasonably expected of an employee. If you want, you can spend the rest of your professional life very comfortably doing these things. Ultimately, you can look forward to getting a couple of small promotions, followed by retirement, followed by death, followed by having your body eaten by insects and bacteria and then excreted in the form of basic chemicals that will serve as fertilizer for unattractive plants with names like "duckweed." Is that what you want?

I didn't think so. Because you're the kind of person who wants to be Number One. Not in the sense of being bacterial excrement, but in the sense of having POWER. We're talking about CLOUT. We're talking about having a staff so large that when you have a dental appointment, you send an aide to get *his* teeth drilled. We're talking about CLAWING YOUR WAY TO THE TOP.

GETTING PROMOTED

You can't expect to get a promotion right away, of course. You should wait two, maybe even three days before you start pushing for it. This will give you time to look around to see who your serious competitors are, to size them up, to evaluate their strengths and weaknesses, and to crush them under the freight elevator.

ATTILA AND BOB

ETHICAL QUESTION: DO YOU HAVE TO BE SCUM TO GET AHEAD?

As the famous baseball codger Leo Durocher was fond of saying before he died: "Nice guys finish last." There is some truth in this. Take the example of Attila the Hun, who was an unpleasant person but an extremely successful Hun, one of the top Huns in the business. His lesser-known brother, Bob the Hun, was a nice guy, but a failure. Bob would show up with this horde outside a medieval village and say, "Listen, would you folks mind if we raped the women and stole everything and killed everybody? You would? Oh my gosh! Sorry!" And off he'd slink, very embarrassed. His was by far the lowest-ranked horde in the league.

But that is just one isolated incident. There are plenty of examples of nice people who DID get to the top. Just look around! There's, ummmm, there's . . . ah, hmmmmm. Ha ha! I'm sure there are *lots* of examples, and for some reason I can't think of a single . . . *wait!* I've got one! Mother Theresa! That's it! Here's a very nice person who nevertheless rose to the top of her profession. So the moral is: even in this dog-eat-dog, highly competitive world, you *can* be a decent human being and still attain a career position where you kneel in the Third-World dirt trying to help the wretched and diseased. But if you want to succeed in a large modern corporation, scum is definitely the way to go.

Okay, let's talk nuts and bolts. In most corporations and organizations, a person gets promoted via a five-step procedure:

1. He works diligently and competently at his job for several years.

2. His superiors gradually start to notice him.

3. Somebody above him in the organization dies, retires, leaves, or is promoted, thus creating an opening.

4. His superiors, after carefully considering all the qualified candidates, promote him.

5. An announcement of the promotion is put up on bulletin boards throughout the building, and his co-workers gather around and pound him on the back (many of them aim for his kidneys).

This procedure is all well and good for most people, but you are not "most people." You are a highly motivated individual who wants to be on the fast track, and you cannot afford to fritter away valuable time working diligently and competently at your job. So your best bet is to skip over steps 1 through 4 and go directly to the only really essential step: the bulletin board announcement. Type it on a quality typewriter, using the format shown here.

That's it! All you have to do now is put it up on the bulletin boards and wait for the congratulations to pour in from your co-workers. Don't let them circle around behind you.

Okay, I know what some of you are thinking. You're thinking: "Dave, doesn't this particular method of career advancement carry with it a certain element of risk?"

I am very pleased to announce that (YOUR NAME) has been promoted to the position of (NAME OF POSITION YOU WOULD LIKE TO BE PROMOTED TO) and will henceforth receive a much larger salary. He will report to me, in the unlikely event he ever has anything to report.

(NAME OF RANDOM VICE-PRESIDENT)

PLEASE POST
ON
Bulletin Board

Yes, it does. For one thing, you have to be very careful about what position you promote yourself to. If you pick a position with a highly specific name such as Auditor, people might expect you to actually "audit" something. You want to pick a position involving words that could mean virtually anything, such as Coordinator and Administrator. If you promote yourself to Coordinating Administrator or Administrative Coordinator, nobody will ever be able to pin an actual job responsibility on you. You can devote full time to deciding on your next promotion.

Another possible problem is: What if your company uses the kind of bulletin boards that are covered by little locked glass doors? What you have to do here is find the person who has the key—this is going to be a low-level employee, of course—and make friends with him and explain that if he will let you use the key, you will promote him to a much, much better job than screwing around with bulletin boards. Like, if your company has a fleet of corporate jets, you could offer to make him a Senior Pilot.

HOW TO ACT LIKE AN EXECUTIVE

As you gradually work your way up through the organization over the course of, let's say, a week, you're going to have to change. You're going to have to become an executive. This means showing maturity, integrity, and leadership. It means having the foresight to know what needs to be done, and the courage to do it. It means not picking your nose in group situations. Did you ever see Lee Iacocca pick *his* nose? Or, for that matter, *anybody*'s nose? Of course not. Lee Iacocca didn't get to be one of the top executives in the history of the world by publicly engaging in personal nasal hygiene. He got there by wearing sharp clothes and smoking expensive cigars. He got there because he had executive *style*. You need to get hold of some, too.

I do not mean to suggest for a moment that all it takes to be a top executive is a custom-tailored European suit. You also need the correct shirt and tie. And for women executives, there is the whole issue of hosiery. This is why I have devoted an entire chapter later in this book to the crucial matter of your wardrobe. But for now we're going to talk about the human side of the executive's job, by which I mean the side where you use humans for various purposes.

DEALING WITH YOUR SUBORDINATES

Always remember this: your subordinates are not machines. They are human beings, with the same needs, the same wants, and the same dreams as you. Okay, maybe not *all* the same dreams. Probably they don't have the one where you're naked in a vat of Yoo-Hoo with the Soviet gymnastics team.

But they want to get ahead, just like you do. They, too, are part of the Carnival of American Capitalism. Like you, they want to reach out from the Carousel of Hard Work to grasp with Brass Ring of Success. And when, after riding 'round and 'round, they finally get their shot at realizing this dream, your job, as a caring and concerned superior, is to give them that extra shove they need to pitch forward off their horses and land headfirst among the Discarded Candied Apple Cores of Failure. Because there are only so many Brass Rings of Success, and you sure as hell don't want a bunch of subordinates barging past you and snatching them all.

So the trick, with subordinates, is to keep them happy, productive, hopeful, and—above all—subordinate. Here's how you do this:

1. MAKE THEM THINK YOU'RE THEIR FRIEND. The way you do this is by engaging in casual office banter with them to indicate that you are Just a Regular Person Who Really Cares for Them as Human Beings. Keep a little file with a three-by-five card for each subordinate, on which you've written personal details such as the subordinate's nickname, hobbies, sex, etc. Review these cards regularly, then go out and make personal remarks to your subordinates:

YOU: Hello, "Bob."
SUBORDINATE: Hello.
YOU (glancing at your three-by-five card):   So! You're still a white male with an interest in photography, eh, "Bob"?
SUBORDINATE: Yes sir.
YOU: Ha ha! Good. Let's engage in casual office banter again sometime soon, "Bob."
SUBORDINATE: Yes sir.
YOU (moving along to next subordinate):   Hello, there, "Chuck." I am very. . .
SUBORDINATE: Excuse me, sir, but my name is Mary. Chuck left last year.
YOU (testily):   Not according to this three-by-five card, he didn't!
SUBORDINATE: Yes sir.

YOU: As I was saying, "Chuck," I am very sorry your wife, Edna, died on October 3, 1981.
SUBORDINATE: Thank you, sir.

2. *GET RID OF THEM IF THEY START COMING UP WITH IDEAS.* Remember the old saying: "A subordinate capable of thinking up an idea is a subordinate capable of realizing that there is no particular reason why he or she should be a subordinate, especially *your* subordinate." This is why dogs are so popular as pets. You can have a dog for its whole lifetime, and it will never once come up with a good idea. It will lie around for over a decade, licking its private parts and always reacting with total wonder and amazement to *your* ideas. "What!?" says the dog, when you call it to the door. "You want me to go *outside!!?* What a *great* idea!!! I *never* would have thought of that!!!"

Cats, on the other hand, don't think you're the least bit superior. They're always watching you with that smartass cat expression and thinking, "God, what a cementhead." Cats are always coming up with their own ideas. They are not team players, and they would make terrible corporate employees. A corporate department staffed by cats would be a real disciplinary nightmare, the kind of department that would never achieve 100 percent of its "fair share" pledge quota to the United Way. Dogs, on the other hand, would go way over the quota. Of course they'd also chew up the pledge cards.

The point I'm trying to make here, as far as I can tell, is that you want subordinates who, when it comes to thinking up ideas, are more like dogs than like cats. Ideally, you should determine this before you hire people, by giving them a test, as explained in the box on page 38.

A DEPARTMENT STAFFED BY CATS WOULD BE A NIGHTMARE.

TEST TO FIND OUT IF A POTENTIAL EMPLOYEE IS THE KIND OF PERSON WHO THINKS UP IDEAS

Show the person three forms, marked A, B, and C. Tell him that part of his job would be to fill out the three forms, then throw Form B away. Stress that this is company policy. If he nods and says, "Okay," or if he asks you a question like, "How can you tell which one is Form B?" hire him. But if he says something like, "Gee, it seems kind of inefficient to fill out a form you're just going to throw away," get rid of him. This is the kind of person who will eventually, no matter how much training you give him, come up with an idea.

You should also check the person's references for telltale statements like: "Ellen comes up with a lot of good ideas." Or: "Ellen is a real innovator." What these people are trying to tell you is: "Ellen will get your job, and you'll wind up on the street licking the insides of discarded chicken gumbo soup cans."

HOW TO FIRE PEOPLE

This is the most painful part of being a supervisor, except for the part when you slam your finger in a file drawer. You never *want* to fire anybody, but sometimes you have an employee who has done something totally unacceptable, such as stealing, or drinking liquor on the job without sharing it, or coming up with an idea, and you have no choice but to let this person go.

There is no good way to fire an employee, but there are some things you can do to make it easier. You can have compassion. You can have understanding. You can have two large security guards named Bruno standing next to you and holding hot knitting needles. Call the employee in and say, "Ted, your performance has been unsatisfactory, so I'm afraid these two Brunos are going to have to poke out your eyes with hot knitting needles. I hate to do this, but the only alternative is to fire you." At this point, Ted will *beg* you to fire him. He may well confess to the Lindbergh baby kidnapping.

That about covers how you should behave around your subordinates. Now for the really important issue, which is

HOW YOU SHOULD BEHAVE AROUND OTHER EXECUTIVES

Years ago, corporation executives tended to be middle-aged white Anglo-Saxon Protestant males with as much individuality, style, and flair as generic denture adhesive. Today's corporations, however, thanks to a growing awareness of the value of diversity and of avoiding giant federal lawsuits, have opened their executive ranks to people of all races and sexes, provided they are willing to act, dress, and talk like middle-aged white Anglo-Saxon Protestant males. This is what you need to learn how to do.

LIST OF TOPICS THAT MIDDLE-AGED WHITE ANGLO-SAXON MALES TALK TO EACH OTHER ABOUT WHEN THEY'RE NOT TALKING BUSINESS

1. SPORTS.

As we can see from the above list, if you want to get along with the other executives, you have to learn how to talk about sports. This is pretty easy, if you know certain key phrases, as shown in the chart.

CHART OF KEY PHRASES TO USE WHEN TALKING ABOUT SPORTS

SPORT	SEASON	KEY PHRASE
FOOTBALL	July to February	"They got some really bad calls."
BASEBALL	March to October	"Some of those calls they got were really bad."
BASKETBALL	August to March	"I can't believe some of those calls they got."
ICE HOCKEY	Eternal	"Can you believe some of those calls they got?"

To you, these phrases may not seem to have a whole lot of meat on them, but believe me, middle-aged white Anglo-Saxon Protestant males can use them to keep a conversation going for hours.

Here's an interesting Ethical Question you might care to think about: If you go to a meeting of executives, and just by chance it happens that not a single one of you is a middle-aged white Anglo-Saxon Protestant male, do you still have to talk about sports? Or could you, in that one meeting, without telling anybody else, switch over to another topic, such as the theater? ("I can't believe some of the reviews they got!")

My personal feeling about this is, it's not worth the risk. Somebody might report you.

JOINING A CLUB

At some point, if you really want to make it to the top, you have to join a club. Actually, you have to join *two* clubs: one should be in the city, and it should be very old and have big dark drafty rooms where deceased members sit and read the paper all day. It should also have really bad food. The idea is, when you want to make a deal with an important client, you take him to your club for lunch, and eventually he realizes that unless the two of you reach an agreement, you'll take him to your club again, so he gives you whatever you want.

The other club is your country club. This is a place where during the day you can relax by putting on ugly pants and golfing with other executives, and at night you can hold social affairs where you give each other golf trophies and, if everybody is in a really funky mood, dance the fox-trot. This is called "networking," and it is very valuable because in the business world, a golf trophy creates a lifelong bond between two people.

Of course most clubs have certain requirements regarding who they will allow to become a member. I don't mean to suggest here that they don't admit minority groups. Ha ha! Don't be ridiculous! After all, these are the eighties! Today's clubs are more than happy to admit any minority person whatsoever, provided this person is also a member of the U.S. Supreme Court. But even if you don't fall into this category, you should apply for membership. What's the worst they can do? Laugh at you? Blow their noses on your application? Foreclose your mortgage? Have you fired and see to it that you'll never again get a job, anywhere in the country, better than Urinal Cake Replacer? Don't be intimidated! Go before the Membership Committee and explain to them that you really, sincerely want to join, and that you will work hard to be the best darned member they have ever had, and that you have photographs of them entering and leaving rooms at the Out-O'-Town Motor Lodge and Motel in various interesting groups of up to six people and two mature female caribou. They'll welcome you with open arms. Don't let them kiss you on the lips.

COMPUTERS IN BUSINESS

You won't last long in the modern business world if you're not comfortable with computers. Computers are involved in every aspect of business from doing the payroll to running the elevators, and if they don't like you, they can make your elevator drop like a stone for 20 floors, then yank it up and drop it again until your skeletal system looks like oatmeal. So you damn well better read this chapter and get comfortable with them and become their friend.

GLOSSARY OF STANDARD
COMPUTER TERMS

BUG. A cute little humorous term used to explain why the computer had your Shipping Department send 150 highly sophisticated jet-fighter servo motors, worth over $26,000 apiece, to fishermen in the Ryuku Islands, who are using them as anchors.

DATA BASE. The information you lose when your memory crashes.

GRAPHICS. The ability to make pie charts and bar graphs, which are the universal business method for making abstract concepts, such as "three," comprehensible to morons like your boss (see page 44).

HARDWARE. Where the people in your company's software section will tell you the problem is.

SOFTWARE. Where the people in your company's hardware section will tell you the problem is.

SPREADSHEET. A kind of program that lets you sit at your desk and ask all kinds of neat "what if?" questions and generate thousands of numbers instead of actually working.

USER. The word that computer professionals use when they mean "idiot."

HOW COMPUTERS WORK

The first computers were big clumsy machines that used vacuum tubes. By today's standards, they were extremely primitive. For example, they believed the sun was carried across the sky on the back of a giant turtle. But the modern computer is much more sophisticated, and far smaller, thanks to a device called the "micro-chip," which, although it is less than one-thousandth the size of a moderate zit, is capable of answering, in a matter of seconds, mathematical questions that would take millions of years for a human being to answer (even longer if he stopped for lunch).

How does the computer do this? Simple. It makes everything up. It knows full well you're not going to waste millions of years checking up on it. So you should never use computers for anything really impor-tant, such as balancing your personal checkbook. But they're fine for corporate use.

HOW TO USE COMPUTER-GENERATED PIE CHARTS AND BAR GRAPHS TO MAKE ABSTRACT CONCEPTS UNDERSTANDABLE TO MORONS LIKE YOUR BOSS

Let's say you have to write a Safety Report. The old-fashioned, pre-computer way to do this would be something like this:

```
In March, we had two people who
got sick because they forgot and
drank coffee from the vending ma-
chine.  Also, Ed Sparge set fire
to his desk again.  Ed has prom-
ised that from now on he will put
his cigar out before he dozes off.
```

But now, using the graphics capability on your computer, you can produce a visually arresting and easy-to-understand report like this:

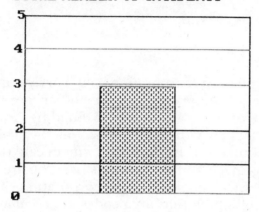

SAFETY REPORT FOR MARCH
TOTAL NUMBER OF INCIDENTS

BREAKDOWN BY CAUSE

Ed setting his desk on fire (33.3%)

People drinking machine coffee (66.7%)

BUSINESS COMMUNICATIONS

No modern corporation can survive unless its employees communicate with each other. For example, let's say that Stan, who works in Building Administration, notices that the safety valve on the main steam boiler is broken. If he doesn't communicate this information to Arnie, over in Maintenance, you are going to have little bits and pieces of the corporation spread out over three, maybe four area codes. So communication is very, very important. It should not, however, be confused with memos.

WHAT MAKES A GOOD BUSINESS MEMO

Ask any business school professor, and he'll tell you a good memo is clear, concise, and well organized. Now ask him what his annual salary is. It's probably less than most top executives spend in a month on shoe maintenance. What you can learn from this is that in your business correspondence, you should avoid being clear, concise, and well organized. Remember the Cardinal Rule of Business Writing (invented by Cardinal Anthony Rule, 1898–1957): "The primary function of almost all corporate correspondence is to enable the writer to avoid personal responsibility for the many major bonehead blunders that constantly occur when you have a bunch of people sitting around all day drinking coffee and wearing uncomfortable clothing."

There are big balloons of blame in every corporation, drifting gently from person to person. The purpose of your memos is to keep these balloons aloft, to bat them gently on their way. This requires soft, meaningless phrases, such as "less than optimal." If you write a direct memo, a memo that uses sharp words such as "bad" to make an actual point, you could burst a balloon and wind up with blame all over your cubicle.

STANDARD FORMAT
FOR THE BUSINESS MEMO

1. ALWAYS START BY SAYING THAT YOU HAVE RECEIVED SOMETHING, AND ARE ENCLOSING SOMETHING. These can be the same thing. For example, you could say: "I have received your memo of the 14th, and am enclosing it." Or they can be two different things: "I have received a letter from my mother, and am enclosing a photograph of the largest-known domestically grown sugar beet." As you can see, these things need have nothing to do with each other, or with the point of the memorandum. They are in your memo solely to honor an ancient business tradition, the

Tradition of Receiving and Enclosing, which would be a shame to lose.

2. STATE THAT SOMETHING HAS BEEN BROUGHT TO YOUR ATTENTION. Never state who brought it. It can be virtually any random fact whatsoever. For example, you might say: "It has been brought to my attention that on the 17th of February, Accounts Receivable notified Collections of a prior past-due balance of $5,878.23 in the account of Whelk, Stoat, and Mandible, Inc." Ideally, your reader will have nothing to do with any of this, but he will think he *should,* or else why would you go to all this trouble to tell him? Also, he will get the feeling you must be a fairly plugged-in individual, to have this kind of thing brought to your attention.

3. STATE THAT SOMETHING IS YOUR UNDERSTANDING. This statement should be firm, vaguely disapproving, and virtually impossible to understand. A good standard one is: "It is my understanding that this was to be ascertained in advance of any further action, pending review."

4. END WITH A STRONG CLOSING LINE. It should leave the reader with the definite feeling that he or she is expected to take some kind of action. For example: "Unless we receive a specific and detailed proposal from you by the 14th, we intend to go ahead and implant the device in Meredith."

The beauty of this basic memo format is that it can even be adapted for sending personalized communications to your subordinates ("It has come to my attention that your wife, Edna, is dead.").

In addition to writing memos, every month or so you should generate a lengthy report. This is strictly so you can cover yourself in case something bad happens.

STANDARD FORMAT TO USE FOR LENGTHY REPORTS TO INSURE THAT NOBODY READS THEM

I. SUBJECT: This is entirely up to you. If you follow the format, it will have virtually no impact on the rest of the report.

II. INTRODUCTION: This should be a fairly long paragraph in which you state that in this report, you intend to explore all the ramifications of the subject, no matter how many it turns out there are.

III. STATEMENT OF PURPOSE: This is a re-statement of the Introduction, only the sentences are in reverse order.

IV. OBJECTIVES: This is a restatement of the Statement of Purpose, only you put the sentences in a little numbered list.

V. INTRODUCTION: By now, nobody will remember that you already had this.

VI. BACKGROUND: Start at the dawn of recorded time.

VII. DISCUSSION: This can be taken at random from the *Encyclopedia Britannica,* because the only people still reading at this point have been able to continue only by virtue of ingesting powerful stimulants and will remember nothing in the morning.

VIII. CONCLUSIONS: You should conclude that your findings tend to support the hypothesis that there are indeed a great many ramifications, all right.

IX. INTRODUCTION: Trust me. Nobody will notice.

X. RECOMMENDATIONS: Recommend that the course of action outlined in the Discussion section (Ha ha! Let them try to find it!) should be seriously considered.

HOW TO WRITE LETTERS

There are various types of letters you write in business, each requiring a different tone.

LETTERS TO CUSTOMERS OR POTENTIAL CUSTOMERS

The basic idea here is to grovel around like a slug writhing in its own slime. For example:

```
Dear Mr. Herckle:

  It certainly was an extremely great
pleasure to fly out to your office in
Butte last week, and even though I didn't
have the enormous gigantic emotional
pleasure of meeting with you in person to
discuss our new product line, I was
certainly extremely pleased and grateful
for the opportunity to squat on your door-
step, and I certainly do want to apologize
for any inconvenience or bloodstains I
may have caused when your extremely impres-
sive dog, Bart, perforated my leg.


Your humble servant,

Byron B. Buffington

Byron B. Buffington
BBB:bbb
```

LETTERS TO COMPANIES
THAT OWE YOUR COMPANY MONEY

In these cases, you want to set a tone that is polite, yet firm:

Dear Mr. Hodpecker:

In going over our records, I note that you have not responded to our invoice of January 12, nor to our reminders of February 9, March 6, April 11, May 4, and June 6; and when we sent Miss Bleemer around to discuss this matter with you personally, you locked her in a conference room with a snake.

Mr. Hodpecker, we of course value your business, and we very much want to keep you as a customer. At least that is what I am trying to tell my two top collection assistants, the Bulemia brothers, Victor and Anthony. They, on the other hand, would prefer to keep you as a pet. They even bought one of those little cages that airlines transport animals in. To me, it looks just barely big enough for a cocker spaniel, but Victor and Anthony believe they can make you fit.

Expecting to hear from you very, very soon in regards to this matter, I remain

Sincerely yours,

Byron B. Buffington

Byron B. Buffington

BBB:ip

P.S. Victor has a complete set of auto-body tools.

LETTERS OF RECOMMENDATION

You have to be thoughtful here. See, *anybody* can get a nice letter of recommendation written about him ("Mr. Hitler always kept his uniform very clean"). So most prospective employers tend to discount what such letters say. This means that to make any kind of impression at all, you must exaggerate violently.

Let's say, for example, you're writing a letter of recommendation for a good employee named Bob, and you tell the simple truth:

"Bob Tucker is by far the best foreman we ever had. He never missed a day of work, got along well with his subordinates, and increased our productivity by 47 percent."

If a prospective employer saw such a ho-hum letter of recommendation, he would naturally assume that Bob was an arsonist child molester. You should spice up the letter with statements such as: "Working on his own time during lunch hour, Bob developed a cure for heart disease." Or: "On at least three separate occasions, Bob sacrificed his life so that others might live."

THE BASIC RULES
OF BUSINESS GRAMMAR

1. USE THE WORD "TRANSPIRE" A LOT.
    Wrong: The dog barked.
    Right: What transpired was, the dog barked.
    Even better: A barking of the dog transpired.

2. *ALSO USE "PARAMETER."*
   Wrong: Employees should not throw paper towels into the toilet.
   Right: Employees should not throw paper towels into the parameters of the toilet.

3. *ALWAYS FOLLOW THE PHRASE "TED AND" WITH THE WORD "MYSELF."*
   Wrong: Ted and I think the pump broke.
   Right: Ted and myself think the pump broke.
   Even better: It is the opinion of Ted and myself that a breakage of the pump transpired.

4. *IF SOMETHING IS FOLLOWING SOMETHING ELSE, ALWAYS LET THE READER KNOW IN ADVANCE VIA THE WORDS: "THE FOLLOWING."*
   Wrong: We opened up the pump and found a dead bat.
   Right: We opened up the pump and found the following: a dead bat.

5. *ALWAYS STRESS THAT WHEN YOU TOLD SOMEBODY SOMETHING, YOU DID IT VERBALLY.*
   Wrong: I told him.
   Right: I told him verbally.

6. *NEVER SPLIT AN INFINITIVE.* An infinitive is a phrase that has a "to" at the beginning, such as "Today, I am going to start my diet." You should not split such a phrase with another word, as in "Today, I am definitely going to start my diet," because it makes you sound insecure about it. It sounds like you know darned well you'll be hitting the pecan fudge before sundown.

7. *NEVER END A SENTENCE WITH A PREPOSITION.* Prepositions are words like "with," "into," "on," "off," "exacerbate," etc. The reason you should never end a sentence with one is that you would be violating a rule of grammar.

> *Wrong:* Youse better be there with the ransom money, on account of we don't want to have to hack nobody's limbs off.
>
> *Right:* . . . on account of we don't want to have to hack off nobody's limbs.
>
> *Even better:* . . . on account of we don't want to have to hack off nobody's limbs with a chain saw.

8. *AVOID DANGLING PARTICIPLES.* A participle is the letters "ing" at the ends of words like "extenuating." You want to avoid having it "dangle" down and disrupt the sentence underneath:

There appear to be some extenuat*ing* circumstances. Ted and myself feel that these   Hey! Get that participle out of here!!

COMMON GRAMMAR QUESTIONS

Q. When's it okay to say "between you and I"?

A. It is correct in the following instance: "Well, just between you and I, the cosmetic surgeon took enough cellulite out of her upper arms to raft down the Colorado River on."

Q. What is the purpose of the apostrophe?

A. The apostrophe is used mainly in hand-lettered signs to alert the reader that an "S" is coming up at the end of a word, as in: WE DO NOT EXCEPT PERSONAL CHECK'S or: NOT RESPONSIBLE FOR ANY ITEM'S. Another important grammar concept to bear in mind when creating hand-lettered signs is that you should put quotation marks around random words for decoration, as in "TRY" OUR HOT DOG'S or even TRY "OUR" HOT DOG'S.

Q. When do you say "who" and when do you say "whom"?

A. You say "who" when you want to find out something, like for example if a friend of yours comes up and says, "You will never guess which of your immediate family members just lost a key limb in a freak Skee-Ball accident," you would reply: "Who?" You say "whom" when you are in Great Britain or you are angry (as in: "And just *whom* do you think is going to clean up after these elk?").

Q. Like many writers, I often get confused about when to use the word "affect" and when to use "infect." Can you help me out?

A. Here is a simple pneumatic device for telling these two similar-sounding words (or "gramophones") apart: Just remember that "infect" begins with "in," which is also how "insect" begins, while "affect" begins with "af," which is an abbreviation for "Air Force."

Q. I have a question concerning the expression: "As far as Fred." I would like to know whether it is preferable to say: "As far as Fred, he always gets the hives from that spicy food"; or, "As far as Fred, that spicy food always gives him the hives."

A. They are both preferable.

Q. What do they mean on the TV weather forecast when they say we are going to have "thundershower activity"?

A. They mean we are not going to have an actual thundershower, per se, but we are going to have thundershower activity, which looks very similar to the untrained eye.

Q. I think my wife is having an affair.

A. I wouldn't doubt it.

MAKING SPEECHES AND ORAL PRESENTATIONS

Most people, no matter how competent they are, break into a cold sweat when they have to speak in public. This is perfectly natural, like being afraid to touch eels. But once you learn a few of the "tricks of the trade" used by professionals, you find it's surprisingly easy, and can even be fun! I'm talking here about eel-touching. Public speaking will always be awful. There are, however, some standard techniques you should be aware of:

1. ACT VERY NERVOUS. A lot of inexperienced speakers try to act cool and confident, which is a big mistake because if your audience thinks you're in control, they'll relax and fall asleep. So you want to keep them on their toes. Have a great big stain under each armpit. Speak in a barely audible monotone. From time to time, stop in mid-sentence and stare in horror at the water pitcher for a full 30 seconds. Try to create the impression in your audience that at any moment they may have to wrestle you to the conference table and force a half dozen Valiums down your throat. After a while, they'll start to feel really sorry for you. They'll help you finish your sentences. At the end, if you ask for questions, the room will be as silent as a tomb. If anybody even starts to ask a question, the others will kick him so hard he may never walk again.

2. *ALWAYS START WITH A JOKE.* Probably the most famous example of a good opening joke is the one Abraham Lincoln used to start the Gettysburg Address. "Four score and seven years ago," he said, and the crowd went nuts. "What the hell is a score?" they asked each other, tears of laughter streaming down their faces.

3. *USE QUOTATIONS FROM FAMOUS DEAD PEOPLE.* You can obtain these in bulk from *Bartlett's Familiar Quotations,* a book of quotations nobody is familiar with.

4. *USE A PIE CHART.* This is pretty much a federal requirement for making a business presentation. It has to have the words "market share."

5. *IF YOU HAVE TO SCRATCH SOMEPLACE LIKE YOUR CROTCH, DRAW THE AUDIENCE'S ATTENTION AWAY FROM YOURSELF VIA A CLEVER RUSE.* Like, you could suddenly point at the window and say, "Hey! What the heck is *that!!??*"

Now let's see how you'd put all these elements together. Suppose you've been called upon to make a presentation to top management from all over the country to explain how come a new product, Armpit Magic Deodorant Soap, is not selling well. Here's what you'd say:

"Good afternoon. A priest and a rabbi are playing golf. The priest hits an incredible shot, and . . .

(30-second pause)

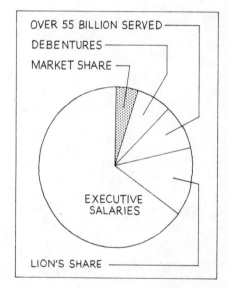

"Staring at this water pitcher, I am reminded of the Bartlett's familiar quotation by the ancient dead Chinese painter, Ku K'ai-Chih, who said: 'Of all kinds of painting, figure painting is the most difficult; then comes landscape painting, and next dogs and horses.'

"But as this pie chart shows . . . *Hey!* What's that over there, away from my crotch!!??

"Ha ha! My mistake. But as this pie chart shows, our 'market share' for Armpit Magic Deodorant Soap is not going to improve in a day, or even two days. It's not going to improve until we figure out some way to make it stop causing the consumer's skin to develop oozing craters the size of Susan B. Anthony dollars. Thank you, and you've been a wonderful audience."

Chapter Six

GIVING GOOD LUNCH

When you're trying to get a prospective client to sign a big contract, it's a good idea to get him away from the formality of the office and into a relaxed dining environment that is more conducive to getting liquored up. But you must select the restaurant carefully: it could destroy the whole effect if his entrée were to arrive in a colorful box festooned with scenes from *Return of the Jedi.* No, you must select a classy restaurant, the kind with valet parking and dozens of apparently superfluous personnel lounging around in tuxedos. You can tell this kind of restaurant by its name.

EXAMPLES OF CLASSY RESTAURANT NAMES	EXAMPLES OF NON-CLASSY RESTAURANT NAMES
Eduardo's	Booger's
La Pleuve en Voiture	The Chew 'n' Swallow
Ye Reallie Olde Countrie Manour Downes Inne	Commander Taco

When you arrive at the restaurant, turn your car over to the youthful narcotics offender in charge of valet parking and promise him a large tip if he doesn't drive it over any preschool children. Now go inside, where you'll be approached by the *maître d'hôtel* (literally, "man who run de hotel"). He will ask: "May I help you?" They're always making this kind of snotty remark.

"NAME-THE-WAITER QUIZ"

WHICH WAITER IS "ERMA MAY"?
WHICH IS "SPUDS"?   WHICH IS "THAD"?

This is where you get to show your prospective client that you have a great deal of *savoir faire* ("five-dollar bills"). Hand the *maître d'* some money. Make sure the prospective client sees this; you might have to snatch it back and hand it over again several times, just to be on the safe side. Then say: "A table for two, my good man." Wink at the prospective client when you say this, so he will realize that you are "slipping" the *maître d'* "a little something" to "grease his palm."

At this point, the *maître d'* may say something like: "But sir, it's 11 A.M. and we don't open for lunch until noon." He is indicating here that he would like several more five-dollar bills. This kind of thing goes on all the time in classy restaurants. Give your prospective client a knowing elbow in his rib cage, then stuff several additional bills into the *maître d's* breast pocket and say: "Oh, I'm sure you can find a table for *us*." Don't quit until he gives you one.

When you are seated, your waiter will arrive with the menus and make the following three statements, all of which are required under the Federal Waitperson Control Act:

1. His name is Thad.

2. It will be His Pleasure to serve you.

3. Would either of you care for a cocktail.

(By the way, this is an ideal opportunity for you to make a witty remark, such as: "What, exactly, is involved in 'caring for' a cocktail? Do they need special food?" This will cause Thad to roar with approving laughter. Tip him $5.)

Now as regards cocktails: the days of the "three-martini lunch" are long gone. In today's high-pressure, brutally competitive business environment, you want a minimum of four martinis, and you want them before the salad comes. Order the same for your prospective client. If he balks, stress that you're paying for them, but that he should not feel obligated because of this.

Now it's time to examine the menu. This requires a great deal of concentration, because you no longer see the simple American menus you knew as a child, which said:

MEAT . . . . $ 5.95

"Fish" or Chicken . . . . . $ 4.95

Spageti . . . . $ 3.95

In those days, you'd mull over the menu for a while, then you'd say, "I'll have the chicken or fish," and the waiter would say, "Excellent choice," and that would be that.

But the modern restaurant menu is much, much more complex, consisting of two or three dozen totally unintelligible items like this:

Les Arbitrages en Console

(Broached Strumpets in Harrow Sauce)

$26.95

Don't panic. Examine your menu carefully, trying not to let on to the prospective client that the only word on it you understand is "Menu" and wait for Thad to return with your drinks. Here's what he'll say:

"Today we are out of everything on the menu, but we do have some very nice specials. For our appetizer, we have an excellent Tête de Chou au Sucre Flambé, which is a head of cabbage covered with sugar and set on fire; we also have a very nice Poisson Sacre Bleu, which is a Norwegian fluke that has been minced into tiny little pieces, then defiled in lemon sauce and stirred until dawn with attractive utensils; we have a superb Coquille St. Jacques au Lanterne, which is a pumpkin stuffed with live writhing scallops; we have a traditional Merde aux Tuilles, which is of course a beef which has been chipped, served with a white sauce on bread which has been toasted; we have a very popular Papier du Oiseau dans la Cage, which is. . . ."

And so on. Thad will keep this up for maybe ten minutes, after which you should tip him $5 and tell him, "I'll have the chicken, and my prospective client here will have whichever menu selection is the most expensive." Stress to the prospective client that this will cost him nothing, as you are paying for it. In fact, it would be a good idea to reassure him on this point several more times during the meal, with such phrases as, "It's on me" and "I'm paying for your food."

After you've ordered from Thad, the wine steward will come around and give you the wine list. The correct wine to select, of course, depends on the kind of entrée you order, as shown in this handy chart:

ENTRÉE	CORRECT WINE
Meat	The appropriate wine here would cost at least $45 a bottle
Fish	With fish you want a bottle of wine costing a minimum of $45
Poultry	You should spend $45 or more for this bottle of wine

If you have trouble remembering all this information, don't worry. Your wine steward will be more than happy to help you make your wine selection:

YOU: How is this wine that costs $12 a bottle?
WINE STEWARD: We use that primarily as a disinfectant.
YOU: I see. Then we'll have something much more expensive.
WINE STEWARD: Excellent choice.

When the steward brings you the wine, he'll show you the label; you should examine it closely for spelling and punctuation errors (see pages 52 to 54, The Basic Rules of Business Grammar). He will then pour a little into your glass. Taste it, and if necessary, have him add a couple of packets of Sweet 'n Low.

At the end of the meal, be sure to make a lighthearted remark about the size of the check, such as: "My God! This check is so large that unless I sign a big contract with a prospective client soon, I'll never be able to afford the operation that will restore the precious gift of sight to my three-year-old daughter, Little Meg, ha ha!" This is your humorous signal to the prospective client that it's time to "talk turkey."

"Ed," you should say (if his name is Ed), "this meal has been a tremendously tax-deductible pleasure for me personally, but let's get down to brass tacks. Looking at this thing objectively, I think it would be a big mistake for you not to sign this contract, especially if you want a ride home." Now give him some time to think it over. Maybe even sprint for the door a couple of times, as if you're running off without him. Better yet, offer to stay there until night falls and buy him dinner. He'll come around.

ENTERTAINING AT HOME

The first question, of course, is: whose home? I think we can rule out *your* home, since, let's be honest here, nobody in your home has ever made a really sincere effort to clean the toilets, and it's far too late to start now. A much better bet would be the client's home. Call him up and explore this possibility with him:

YOU: Ed, Denise and I are wondering if you and Trudy would be free to have dinner with us at your home Friday night.
CLIENT: What?
YOU: How are your toilets?
CLIENT: What?
YOU: Cleaner than ours, I bet!
CLIENT: You want to have dinner at *our home?*
YOU: Sounds good to me! Eight o'clock Friday it is!

You should arrive a bit early, say fiveish, to rummage around and make sure there's plenty of pre-dinner liquor on hand. When Ed and Trudy come out of their bedroom, your first responsibility is to make them feel at ease. I suggest you get a copy of the *Complete Book of Games and Stunts* published in MCMLVI by Bonanza Books and authored by Darwin A. Hindman, Ph.D., professor of physical education at the University of Missouri. This is an actual book, available at garage sales everywhere. I especially recommend the "Funnel Trick" described in chapter 4 ("Snares"), wherein you have the victim lean his head back and place a penny on his forehead, then you tell him that the object of the trick is to tilt his head forward so the penny drops into a funnel stuck into his belt.

However—get this—while he's got his head tilted back, you pour a pitcher of water into the funnel and get his pants soaking wet! Ha ha! Be sure to follow this with a lighthearted remark ("You look like a cretin, Ed!") and offer everybody a swig from the liquor bottle.

Now that everybody is loosened up, drop a hint ("God I'm hungry! Any food around here?") that it's time to move to the dinner table. Your goal at dinner, of course, is to somehow cause the prospective client to get a wad of food caught in his throat and start choking, so you can leap up and dislodge the food by means of the "Heimlich maneuver," thus causing the client to be indebted to you for the rest of his life. This means you have to startle him just as the food is going down his throat. The most reliable way to do this is to have a pistol hidden under the table, and fire it off just as he starts to swallow. You should of course use blanks, as bullets would be irresponsible.

THE HEIMLICH MANEUVER

Stand behind the victim and put your arms around him. Make a fist with one hand and grab it with the other, then yank your hands sharply into the victim's abdomen, thus causing the wad of food to be expelled.

HEIMLICH-MANEUVER HOCKEY

Have two opposing players, each holding a victim, stand about six feet apart. Each player tries to expel his victim's food wad into the other victim's mouth.

WHAT TO DO IF A CLIENT OR BUSINESS ASSOCIATE DIES

Send a flower arrangement that does *not* have little pink or blue rattles in it. Wear black clothes to the funeral. If you don't have black clothes, wear the darkest clothes you have. Tiptoe up to the next of kin during the service and explain this fact to them. "These are the darkest clothes I have," you should say, taking care to whisper. Next you should tell them how awful you feel. "God!" you should say. "I feel terrible! Just horrible!"

Next you should go up and examine the deceased, then go back and inform the next of kin how good he looks. "Ed looks great!" you should say. "You can hardly even tell he's dead!" Unless Ed is in an urn.

INAPPROPRIATE

APPROPRIATE

Chapter Seven

HOW TO DRESS EXACTLY LIKE EVERYBODY ELSE

Take a moment to consider the way the world's truly successful people dress. They dress like mental patients. Your prime example is Prince Charles. Here is one of the world's top princes, if not *the* top prince, yet he is constantly showing up in public wearing ludicrous Sergeant Pepper-style outfits featuring hats with enormous feathers. Or you'll see a picture of him visiting some remote fungal nation and cheerfully wearing ritual native vegetation around his neck. There are plenty of other examples of highly successful people who dress absurdly: Mick Jagger, the Joint Chiefs of Staff, and Ronald McDonald, to name just three. And of course you can't find a really successful world religious leader who doesn't wear a comical outfit.

So what does this tell you about how you should dress if you want to succeed in American business? Nothing. Because the way we dress in American business is not based on the way the world's truly successful people dress. It is based on the way John T. Molloy says we should dress. Molloy is the author of the best-selling books *Dress for Success, The Woman's Dress for Success Book, Live for Success,* and *Success in the Afterlife.* He openly admits to practicing a science called "wardrobe engineering." He has done extensive wardrobe research, wherein he tested the reactions of thousands of groups of people to the way different individuals were dressed. What he found, after years and years of study, was that the groups always liked it best when the individuals were naked. So he pretty much gave up the research and decided instead to author best-selling books containing incredibly detailed instructions on how to dress and what accessories to carry, instructions that were so slavishly followed by the business community that they briefly resulted in a worldwide shortage of Cross pens.

The bottom line is, if you truly want to present a business wardrobe image that makes the all-important fashion statement: "I look exactly like everybody else in American business," you damn well better dress the way John T. Molloy says you should. So listen up.

HOW MEN SHOULD DRESS

Basically, the American businessman should dress as though he recently lost his entire family in a tragic boat explosion. We are talking about a subdued look here. This doesn't mean that you have no choice in what you wear. Au contraire.* For example, you may wear two completely different colors of woolen suit: you may wear a dark gray woolen suit, or, if you want to get really crazy, you may wear a dark blue woolen suit.

You may *not* wear a brown, green, or (God forbid) plaid polyester suit, because everybody will think you just tromped into town from rural Louisiana to attend the Live Bait Show. Men wearing these colors are very likely to be passed over for promotion, as is shown by this actual simulation of a scene that for all we know probably occurs every day in major corporations:

(We are in the office of the president, who is meeting with a vice-president to decide whom to promote to director of the Research Department.)

*"Ah, that country air."

VICE-PRESIDENT: Well, there's Barkley, of course. He's the one who came up with the way to turn discarded wads of Kleenex into gold using only common household ingredients.
PRESIDENT: What color suit does he wear?
VICE-PRESIDENT: Brown.
PRESIDENT: Well forget *him*.

SHIRTS

Your shirt should be white, and it should not have the name "Earl" embroidered anywhere on it.

TIES

The purpose of your tie is to suggest that you attended an Ivy League university, so the key is to select the right pattern, as shown here.

HOW TO TIE A TIE

Face southwest, with the long end of the tie hanging down casually from your right hand (the audience's left hand). Now bring the short end of the tie around the back of your neck and let it hang down your front, so that it just touches the scar you got ironing shirts naked. Now take the "wide" (or "long") end of the tie and pass it three times around the "short" (or "long") end, then up through the loop. (What do you mean, "What loop?" Check again!) Now pull everything snug, unless you have forgotten to put on a shirt, in which case you had best remove the tie, by force if necessary.

SHOES

These are a "must" in most business situations. If you use "Odor Eaters," they should be beige or navy blue.

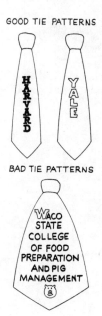

GOOD TIE PATTERNS

HARVARD   YALE

BAD TIE PATTERNS

WACO STATE COLLEGE OF FOOD PREPARATION AND PIG MANAGEMENT

POWER UNDERWEAR PATTERNS

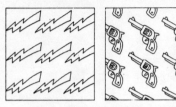

STRONG   VERY STRONG

LEE IACOCCA'S PERSONAL
UNDERWEAR PATTERN

FIGURE 1   FIGURE 2

UNDERWEAR

No area of the male business wardrobe is as important as his underwear. Next time you're in a room with a group of successful executives, take a few moments to examine their underwear, and you'll find they're all wearing underwear with proven "power patterns" that have been shown in scientific tests to create a feeling of awe and respect in others.

In situations where you really need to enhance your power image, you should wear your power underwear *outside* your pants (figure 1). In extreme situations, such as you are arguing before the U.S. Supreme Court, you will want to wear them in an even more visible location, such as on your head (figure 2).

HOW WOMEN SHOULD DRESS

In deciding how to dress for business, women must understand certain basic facts, the foremost being that all men are scum. If a woman, no matter how competent, gives off the slightest hint that she has any feelings that could be remotely construed as sexual, this is all that the men in her corporation will ever think about. That's not just my opinion: it is a scientific finding based on years of extensively hanging around with guys and talking.

What does this mean, in terms of your business wardrobe? It means you want to adopt a fashion look that has become the standard for the woman on the corporate fast track, a look that can best be described as: Modified Nun. As you can see from the illustration on page 71, all we've really done to the basic nun look is remove the headpiece. This conveys to the men in your corporation that you are not a sex object, but an authority figure who must be taken seriously because at any moment you might strike them on the hands with a ruler.

HOSIERY

This is mandatory. I realize you women hate to be constantly shelling out money for a product manufactured by an industry that pays its scientists huge bonuses if they can develop fibers even weaker than the ones they currently use. I realize you go around saying: "If we can land a man on the moon, why can't we develop pantyhose that will last longer than a small vanilla cone on a hot day?" Well I'm sorry, but rules are rules. Also, we haven't landed a man on the moon for a very long time now, and we probably never will again unless something urgent comes up, such as the Defense Department suspects there are Cuban troops up there.

MAKEUP

A good rule of thumb is: if you can stick a pin more than a quarter inch into your face and still not feel anything, you're wearing too much makeup for the business environment. Or else you have a medical problem.

SHOES

The ideal shoe for the career woman is the basic pump with a "sensible" heel, by which I mean a heel that will just fit through the holes in a standard street grate.

NUN   BUSINESSWOMAN

Chapter Eight

SALES

What makes a good salesperson? In an effort to answer that question, I asked my research associates to interview the top 100 salespeople, based on dollar volume, in the nation. Naturally, my associates refused to do this. I wouldn't have done it either. Life is hard enough without voluntarily subjecting yourself to top salespeople.

What we can learn from this research is that if you want to become a top salesperson, you must develop drive, determination, and persistence such that people do not wish to be within thousands of yards of you. How can you become this kind of person? By BELIEVING IN YOURSELF. You must develop a FAITH IN YOUR OWN ABILITIES so strong that YOU DON'T FEEL THE LEAST BIT EMBARRASSED ABOUT ACTING LIKE A SCUZZBAG. You don't get this kind of confidence from other people; it has to COME FROM WITHIN, from having a comprehensive, meaningful, and deep-rooted PHILOSOPHY OF LIFE based on TIMELESS TRUTHS, which you get from MOTIVATIONAL BOOKS THAT ARE ALSO AVAILABLE ON CASSETTE TAPES COSTING $49.95 PER SET.

Without question, the number-one cassette thinker in the world today is Dr. Lance M. Canker, the man whose famous motivational tape "Dare to Be a Jerk" is believed to be the single biggest factor in the historic decision by Coca-Cola executives to change the

Coke formula so it tasted more like children's cough syrup. Dr. Canker, who has had a lifelong interest in motivational thinking ever since 1963, when he had his name legally changed from "Lance Canker" to "Dr. Lance Canker," has written a number of self-help books, including the hugely popular *God, Are You Fat!* But his greatest contribution to the business world is his classic how-to-sell book *Buy This Book or You'll Starve to Death,* which is filled with true-life inspirational anecdotes such as these:

> Not long ago, I gave a dinner party attended by every major Western head of state and a young man I'll call "Jon." Although he is attractive, intelligent, and talented, "Jon" was a very unhappy person, and he was thinking of killing himself. So I took him aside. " 'Jon,' " I said. "Lighten up." Today, he is the president of General Motors.
>
> Not long after that, I got a telephone call from a major world religious leader, whom I'll call "the Pope." Although he is attractive, intelligent, and talented, he was feeling tremendous anxiety about the fate of mankind. "Hey," I advised him. "Forget it." And today he, too, is the president of General Motors.

Using proven techniques such as these, Dr. Canker shows in *Buy This Book or You'll Starve to Death* how any member of the vertebrate family can develop powerful selling skills. In this chapter, we shall draw extensively on the information contained in Dr. Canker's book, and by the time Dr. Canker finds out about this, we shall be long gone.

RULE #1: MAINTAIN EYE CONTACT WITH THE PROSPECT AT ALL TIMES NO MATTER WHAT

This is extremely important. If the prospect tries to glance out the window, you must race over and stand in front of the window. If you hand him a document and he attempts to read it, you must place your head between the document and his eyes. If he goes to the bathroom, you must maintain eye contact as best you can from the adjacent stall or urinal. This may make you uncomfortable, especially if you and the prospect happen to belong to differing sexes, but if you don't do it, you'll give the impression that you're not being totally honest and you don't truly believe in your product, whatever the hell it is.

COMMON QUESTION #1: What if the prospect is blind?
ANSWER: Then you must maintain *knee* contact.

COMMON QUESTION #2: Well, what if the prospect is blind *and* has a wooden leg?
ANSWER: Well, then you would . . .

COMMON QUESTION #3: Also he's in a coma.
ANSWER: Hey! *These* aren't common questions!

RULE #2: CALL THE PROSPECT BY HIS FIRST NAME A LOT, BECAUSE HE MIGHT FORGET YOU'RE TALKING TO HIM

WRONG: "Bob, have you ever given any thought as to who would provide for the financial security of your wife and children if, God forbid, you were to be killed by falling cement?"

RIGHT: "Bob, have you, Bob, ever given any thought as to who would provide for the financial security of your, Bob's, wife and children if you, Bob, were to be killed by falling cement, Bob? Huh? Bob?"

RULE #3: LEARN TO READ THE PROSPECT'S "BODY LANGUAGE"

If you've ever driven on the Long Island Expressway, you know that people often communicate to each other "nonverbally," which means rather than using words, they use fingers, arm gestures, facial expressions, teeth, knives, etc. As a smart salesperson, you must learn to "read" the prospect's body language so you can take appropriate action, such as shielding your face.

RULE #4: GET THE PROSPECT INTO A "YES" FRAME OF MIND

The way you do this is by making a series of statements that the prospect cannot help but agree with. Let's listen in to this actual transcript of a top salesperson applying this technique:

SALESPERSON: Hi, Bob! Great to see you! Bob, I want to thank you for giving me an appointment. Bob.
PROSPECT: I didn't give you an appointment. You got in here by sedating my receptionist with chloroform.
SALESPERSON: Ha ha! Bob, Bob, Bob. I can't put anything over on you, can I? But seriously, Bob, wouldn't you agree that Adolf Hitler was a bad person?
PROSPECT: Well, yes, but I . . .
SALESPERSON: And don't you feel, Bob, that child abuse is wrong?
PROSPECT: Of course. Sure. I mean . . .

BODY LANGUAGE POSITIONS

PROSPECT IS SAD

PROSPECT HAS AN AXE

PROSPECT IS SURROUNDED BY GIANT BIRDS, SOME OF WHICH HAVE TEETH

PROSPECT HAS JUMPED OUT THE WINDOW

SALESPERSON (swinging a watch back and forth rhythmically on a chain):   And would it not be correct to state, Bob, that in a right triangle, the square of the hypotenuse equals the sum of the squares of the other two sides?
PROSPECT (getting drowsy):   Whatever you say.

At this point, if you have the prospect in a positive enough mood, you may be able to simply take his wallet. Otherwise you should go on to Rule #5.

RULE #5: ASK FOR THE SALE

Be direct. Something like: "Bob, how about a large order for whatever it is I'm selling?"

Usually the prospect will balk, offering any one of a number of standard excuses, such as:

• "I want to think about it."
• "I want to talk to my husband or wife about it, depending on what sex I am."
• "Get out of my sight before I kill you and feed your pancreas to rats."

This is normal sales resistance, and you must not let it faze you. Go back and repeat your presentation, very slowly, starting with "Hi, Bob! Great to see you, Bob!" Try to get the prospect to voice specific objections so you can overcome them ("Are you saying, Bob, that you think Adolf Hitler was *not* a bad person?"). Do this as many times as necessary, until Bob comes around. Remind him that if he doesn't, you may have to take him to Lunch (see chapter 6).

Chapter Nine

HOW TO GO INTO BUSINESS FOR YOURSELF

The story of America is the story of individuals—the Henry Fords, the John DeLoreans, the Speedy Alka-Seltzers, the Don Corleones—who started out alone, with little more than a dream and a willingness to work toward it, and ended up running large organizations and eventually either dying or getting indicted. Chances are that you, too, have an idea for a business percolating inside you, an idea you're sure would work, if only you gave it a chance.

Well, why not? What, really, are you getting from your company job, aside from a steady paycheck, regular raises, job security, extensive medical benefits, and a comfortable pension? Hey, if *that's* all they think you're worth, well, in the words of the popular country-and-western song: "Take This Job and Let Me Hold onto It while I Start My Own Little Business on the Side."

Step one is to find out what legal requirements you have to meet to register yourself as a small business. In most states, this is a two-part process:

1. You have several boxes of cheap business cards printed up with the wrong phone number.

2. You go around and pin your card onto those bulletin boards you see in supermarkets and low-rent restaurants, the ones with 10,000 other business cards that look like the one shown here.

Stuart A. Caliper
Accounting and Light Masonry
"Since April 3, 1986, at about 4:30"

TAX IMPLICATIONS OF GOING INTO BUSINESS FOR YOURSELF

The tax implications are that you can deduct every nickel you ever spend for the rest of your life, including on bowling accessories (see chapter 10, How Finance Works).

THREE SUREFIRE BUSINESS CONCEPTS

Over the years, I have thought up several business concepts that are so obviously brilliant that the only way they could conceivably fail would be if somebody actually tried them. This is where you fit in. Pick any one of the concepts below and invest your life savings in it. If you are not completely satisfied that the concept was not all that I said it was, if not more, then you do not owe me a cent. Sound too good to be true? Well just wait until you see these concepts!

CONCEPT #1: THE ELECTRIC APPLIANCE SUICIDE MODULE

This concept is based on the known fact that it is impossible to get electronic devices repaired. Let's say you have purchased a videocassette recorder, and after a while, because of normal wear and tear such as your nephew Dwight stuck a Polish sausage into the slot and pushed the fast forward button, it stops working.

Now you have two options. One is to take it back to the store where you got it, which will send it back to the "Factory Service Center." Here's what I have to say about this option: Hahahahahahaha. Because the "Factory Service Center" is in fact a giant warehouse containing hundreds of thousands of broken electronic devices, including 1952 Philco television sets. The staff consists of two elderly men, named Roscoe and Lester, who will poke around inside your VCR with cheap cigars and go, "Lookit all them *wires* in there!"

Your other choice is to take it to a local "repair shop," which will consist of a sullen person standing behind a counter with an insulting sign like the one shown here.

Obviously, neither of these is an acceptable option. So the logical thing to do, when an electronic device breaks, is to just throw it away and get another one, right? But you can't bring yourself to do this. You paid $700 for it, and you'd feel guilty. So you put yourself in the hands of incompetents and thieves.

This is where the Electric Appliance Suicide Module would come in. It would be a device costing $29.95 and consisting of a small, powerful explosive charge, coupled to a tiny electronic "brain," which the consumer would implant inside his VCR or television set via a simple procedure requiring only a screwdriver and three beers. They way the Suicide Module would work is, as soon as the brain sensed that the appliance was no longer working properly, it would set off the charge. For safety reasons, this would occur in the middle of the night, when the consumers were asleep. The consumer would be awakened by a large BLAM!! in his living room, and he'd come rushing out, and there, where his television set used to be, he'd see a grayish cloud of vaporized plastic, and he'd say: "Huh! Time to get a new TV!" Besides eliminating a lot of consumer guilt, the Suicide Module would probably provide a very powerful incentive for appliances to perform well. They would work their little diodes to the bone, for fear that otherwise the Suicide Module might think they were starting to come down with something.

CONCEPT #2: THE "MISTER MEDIOCRE" FAST-FOOD RESTAURANT FRANCHISE

I have studied American eating preferences for years, and believe me, this is what people want. They don't want to go into an unfamiliar restaurant, because they don't know whether the food will be very bad, or very good, or what. They want to go into a restaurant that advertises on national television, where they *know* the food will be mediocre. This is the heart of the Mister Mediocre concept.

The basic menu item, in fact the only menu item, would be a food unit called the "patty," consisting of—this would be guaranteed in writing—"100 percent animal matter of some kind." All patties would be heated up and then cooled back down in electronic devices immediately before serving. The Breakfast Patty would be a patty on a bun with lettuce, tomato, onion, egg, Ba-Ko-Bits, Cheez Whiz, a Special Sauce made by pouring ketchup out of a bottle, and a little slip of paper stating: "Inspected by Number 12." The Lunch or Dinner Patty would be any Breakfast Patties that didn't get sold in the morning. The Seafood Lover's Patty would be any patties that were starting to emit a serious aroma. Patties that were too rank even to be Seafood Lover's Patties would be compressed into wads and sold as "Nuggets." Any nuggets that had not been sold as of the end of the month would be used to make bricks for new Mister Mediocre restaurants.

CONCEPT #3: THE "BINGO THE LEECH" LICENSED CHARACTER

If you have young children, you know how they tend to develop powerful attachments, similar to cocaine addiction only more expensive, to the toy industry's many lovable and imaginative licensed characters such as (for girls) Rainbow Brite, Strawberry Shortcake, Wee Whiny Winkie, The Dweebs, and The Simper Sisters; and (for boys) He-Man, The Limb Whackers, The Eye Eaters, Sergeant Bicep, and Testosterone Bob's Hurt Patrol. Once a child gets one of these characters, he or she suddenly just *has* to have all the others in the set, plus the accessories, all of which are—believe me when I tell you this—Sold Separately.

BINGO THE LEECH

So I have come up with this concept for a truly irresistible licensed character named Bingo the Leech. Bingo would be an adorable little stuffed leech with big loving eyes and a tube of industrial quick-drying epoxy concealed in his lips. When a child picked up Bingo at the store and squeezed him, Bingo would emit some epoxy and become permanently bonded to the child's skin, and the parent would have to buy him so as to avoid shoplifting charges. Then the parent would have to buy all the other members of the Bingo family, because only by combining their lip secretions would you obtain the antidote chemical required to get Bingo off the child before it was time to go to college.

Chapter Ten

HOW FINANCE WORKS

WHO SHOULD READ THIS CHAPTER

At some point in your rise to the top, you may find yourself appointed to a job where you have to know something about finances, such as as Controller or Treasurer or Chairman of the Federal Reserve Board. If this happens, you should read this chapter. But I warn you: this stuff is deadly dull, as is illustrated by accountants. You never hear people say: "Let's have some *fun* tonight! Let's go find some *accountants!*" So unless you have no choice, you should skip this chapter. I myself am going to require powerful illegal stimulants to write it.

HOW CORPORATE FINANCES WORK

You look at a big corporation, with giant expensive buildings filled with tasteful carpets and big desks and rental plants and well-paid employees making Xerox-brand copies of the crossword puzzle, and you wonder, "How on earth do they make any money?"

The answer is, they don't. They lose money hand over fist. Read the business section of any newspaper, and just about every day you'll see a story like the one reproduced at left.

The reason these executives can afford to be so cavalier is that they know they can always get more money—any amount, any time—by means of a process so simple you are going to laugh when I tell you about

DETROIT—The General Motors Corporation reported today that it lost $64.6 million in the first fiscal quarter. "We have no idea what happened to the money," said top GM officials, in unison. "One moment it was lying on the dresser, and the next moment it was gone! We could just kick ourselves! Ha ha!"

it, unless you have already fallen asleep at this point. All they have to do is print up some "stock." A stock is basically a piece of high-quality paper, similar to what certificates of appreciation from bowling leagues are printed on, except it has a nice border and a statement such as the following printed on it in an attractive and historic type style:

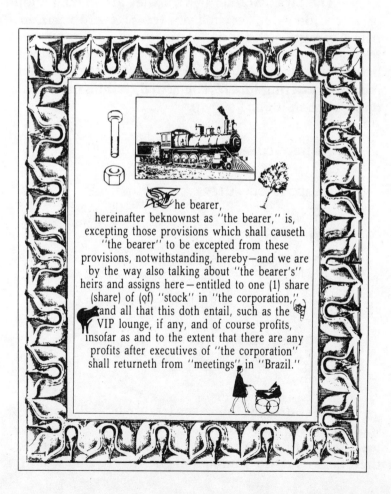

T he bearer, hereinafter beknownst as "the bearer," is, excepting those provisions which shall causeth "the bearer" to be excepted from these provisions, notwithstanding, hereby—and we are by the way also talking about "the bearer's" heirs and assigns here—entitled to one (1) share (share) of (of) "stock" in "the corporation," and all that this doth entail, such as the VIP lounge, if any, and of course profits, insofar as and to the extent that there are any profits after executives of "the corporation" shall returneth from "meetings" in "Brazil."

Now you're thinking: "Yes, but who would be so stupid as to exchange money for this piece of paper?" Well, I realize it makes very little sense to a person of normal intelligence, but it turns out there is a major financial institution devoted to this very purpose.

THE STOCK MARKET

The Stock Market is what they are talking about on television when they tell you the "Dow Jones Industrial Average" is "up" in "active trading." Sometimes they show you a picture of it: you see a lot of men with bad armpit stains yelling and waving their arms. These men are ordering lunch. The actual trading of stocks is done by computers:

```
FIRST COMPUTER: HOW MUCH YOU WANT
FOR THOSE 20 SHARES OF STOCK

SECOND COMPUTER: THESE ARE VERY
NICE SHARES AND BECAUSE WE ARE
FRIENDS I MAKE FOR YOU A SPECIAL
DEAL $600

FIRST COMPUTER: YOU CALL ME A
FRIEND AND HERE YOU ARE STAB-
BING ME IN THE BACK THESE SHARES
I WOULD NOT FEED TO A GOAT $400
IS THE BEST I CAN DO

SECOND COMPUTER: $550 IS THE
LOWEST I CAN GO MAY GOD STRIKE
ME DEAD IF I AM LYING
```

Of course all this takes less than a billionth of a second. At the end of the day, the computers divide the total prices of all stocks sold by the number of stocks, then they take the numbers of the horses that won the first three races, and. . . . No, wait a minute. That's the "Trifecta" I'm thinking of. Well, somehow, they figure out the Dow Jones Industrial Average, and they tell the television news people about it.

COMMON FINANCIAL QUESTIONS

Q. What makes one corporation's stock more valuable than another one?

A. The most important factor is what kind of hors d'oeuvre the corporation serves at its Annual Stockholders Meeting, which is when all the stockholders get invited to a hotel ballroom to hear highly paid executives attempt to explain how come the corporation is making less of a profit than it would if it had just sold all of its factories and machines and put the money in Christmas Clubs. If the corporation serves a cheap hors d'oeuvre, such as crackers and cheese, its stock will drop; if it switches over to, say, shrimp, the stock will rise. Of course the people on Wall Street don't want to admit this, which is why they're always making up preposterous explanations as to why stock prices rise and fall, such as "tension in the Middle East," when of course there is *always* tension in the Middle East. When we finally have a nuclear war and there is no life left on Earth except cockroaches, the cockroaches in the Middle East will be tense.

Q. Who is "Dow Jones"?
A. A dead person.

Q. What is the "options" market?
A. This is a special market for people who are too stupid even to buy stocks. The way it works is, let's

say a farmer or somebody realizes he has 500 pork bellies. Now I think we can all agree that no sane person would want to have even *one* pork belly, let alone 500 of them, so what this farmer does is look around for the stupidest person he can find, and he sells him a pork-belly "future," which means that the stupid person gives the farmer some money and agrees to take delivery of the pork bellies at a later date. I know you think I'm making this up, but believe me, people actually do this.

When the stupid person realizes what he has done, he of course tries to find an even stupider person to buy the "future," and this person sells it to an even stupider person, and so on until the big day arrives and a person with no discernible brain whatsoever has 500 pork bellies dumped on his lawn and is immediately arrested by the Board of Health.

AFTERWORD

And so, here you are. Just a dozen or so chapters ago, you were a recent graduate or some other kind of low-life scum, and now, thanks to this book, look what you have become! A highly paid corporate executive! Or a convicted felon!

I do not ask for your gratitude. I seek no reward. No, for me it is enough simply to know that I have, in some small way, helped to make you the kind of executive who can provide much-needed leadership as the corporation of today faces the challenges of tomorrow; the kind of executive who will not be afraid to meet these challenges head-on by means of innovative and far-reaching new management techniques such as bringing me in as a consultant for $2,000 per day plus lunch money. I'll be calling you real soon.